APOCALYPSE
2070

GENE and DOROTHY NEILL

APOCALYPSE 2070

Copyright © 2016 by Dorothy Neill

ISBN: 978-0-9858196-5-1

Scripture quotations are taken from:

English Standard Version Bible with Apocrypha copyright © 2001 by Crossway Bibles, a publishing ministry of Good News Publishers. The Apocrypha, copyright © 2009 by Oxford University Press, Inc., New York, NY 10016. Used by permission. All rights reserved.

Revised Standard Version of the Bible, Apocrypha, copyright 1957; The Third and Fourth Books of the Maccabees and Psalm 151, copyright 1977 by the Division of Christian Education of the National Council of the Churches of Christ in the United States of America. Used by permission. All rights reserved.

Where italics or bold face type are utilized for emphasis in the Scriptures quoted, these are the authors' accents and do not appear in the versions from which they are taken.

Much of the content of this book is taken from a previously published Ebook (2012) by the authors entitled No More Beyond 2070. Apocalypse 2070 has been modified and updated.

COVER DESIGN VOTI, TN

TABLE OF CONTENTS

PREFACE

Although Revelation is the last book of the Christian Bible and almost entirely devoted to the prophetic mysteries surrounding the end times, it is actually the culmination of well over 5,000 years of prophecies concerning the cataclysmic times which will shortly bring about the end of the world and the total destruction of mankind.

The Great Tribulation, more commonly referred to in Scripture as the wrath of God or the Day of the Lord, has been the stuff of endless speculation, false prophecy - and false interpretation of prophecy - since John wrote Revelation 2,000 years ago. Those few saints (Moses, Abraham, Esra (or Ezdras) and other Old Testament prophets) to whom God periodically revealed some of the secrets of "Armageddon" - *the great end-time battle of Right against Wrong* - did not usually divulge what they were told simply because the time had not yet come for these things to be known.

But today, the long-prophesied signs of the apocalypse - "doomsday" to some - are well underway. The day of the beast of Revelation - sometimes erroneously referred to as "the antichrist" - who causes all of mankind to receive "the mark of the beast," is already visible on the horizon. And the secrets of the eschatological mysteries which God once cloaked in enigmatic rhetoric are now revealed within the pages of this book - **APOCALYSE 2070**.

". . . among the mature we do impart wisdom, although it is not a wisdom of this age. . . . But we impart a secret and hidden wisdom of God. . . . For the spirit searches everything, even the depths of God. . . . Now we have received not the spirit of this world, but the spirit which is from God, that we might understand the gifts bestowed on us by God.

And we impart this in words not taught by human wisdom but taught by the Spirit, interpreting spiritual truths to those who possess the Spirit. The unspiritual man does not receive the gifts of the Spirit of God, for they are folly to him, and he is not able to understand them because they are spiritually discerned."

I Cor. 2:6,7,10,12-14

LONG AGO AND FAR AWAY

Most maps don't even show the tiny island of Patmos. Lost in a maze of a thousand other little chunks of rock and sand, Patmos is just one more of the whitewashed Greek islands jutting abruptly out of the Aegean Sea. Immutable. Enchanted. A cobblestone never-never land, she is wrapped in her own poignant world of antiquity. In an age long forgotten by most, a wise old fisherman named John trod the wave-torn beaches there, his snow-white hair flowing in the gentle sea breeze. Deeply tanned, he squinted out under the blazing Mediterranean sun to the southeast and occasionally smiled a tear at thoughts of friends long gone

Most history books record him very briefly – if at all. He was the closest friend of a man called Jesus of Nazareth.

John wrote his book there on Patmos almost two thousand years ago, but he never gave it a title. The revered scholars of yore dramatically named it The Revelation of Jesus Christ to St. John the Divine.

Every single word of John's Revelation – and of this book which you are about to read – is absolutely true. Whether you believe it or not is immaterial. Whether you are going to be one of the few who live through it is quite another matter.

But John was long ago and far away, and time has now forged its relentless path through the centuries.

Today it is the year 2069

We are in the city of Los Angeles, California. Ironically, The City of Angels.

"Spring" is what we once called this season. A time when flowers and love blossomed. But today a cataclysmic silence cries out its final death gasp across this once throbbing city. There is no sound save that of sporadic gunfire. Dead vines blanket the freeways where once behemoth tractor-trailer rigs belched forth their ghastly pall of black, and millions of mindless commuters roared their senseless ways to nowhere. A society where fornication and homosexuality were subsidized by the government, but where it was illegal for school children to pray.

And around the world the scene is the same. Mexico City, once the largest megalopolis on earth, lies in ruins, inhabited only by what few vultures and rats are left.

There is no London. Or Paris. Only dark funeral requiems of terror and agony. Dirges of a society which long ago turned its back on God.

Today the seas are dead; the trees and grass are burnt; the stars are gone; and blackened skies hang like death shrouds over empty cities.

The Four Horsemen of the Apocalypse have ridden their ghastly ride!

No amount of gold will buy a loaf of bread, and ravenous packs of starving psychotics cannibalize what little is left of the world.

The rhinestone televangelists and carnival "faith healers" prattle now only in the darkness of their unmarked graves. And the humanistic priests and pastors – those false shepherds who slept while their flocks wandered and perished – now preach their silent sermons in the halls of impious Death. The few true Christians left on earth have banded securely together in small groups, hidden high up in the mountains and on remote islands of the sea. Self-sustaining, at peace, away from all else.

Gene and Dorothy Neill

GENE AND DOROTHY NEILL

CHAPTER ONE

IN THE BEGINNING

As though there were not enough conflicts in the Middle East, Orthodox Israeli religious leaders seemed about to start a unique war of their own a couple of decades ago. The unlikely target of their hostilities weighed in at seven to eight tons, was some fifty feet long, and had been dead for 65 million years.

Inspired by Steven Spielberg's movie, *Jurassic Park,* a mega box office hit about dinosaurs, likenesses of these prehistoric creatures started popping up everywhere around the world – on key chains, bumper stickers, hamburger boxes, and even on milk containers. One dairy in Israel launched a nationwide marketing campaign using dinosaurs to promote their dairy products. But Aguda Israel, an ultra-Orthodox organization, demanded the dairy withdraw the ads or lose their Glatt Kosher certification.

Orthodox Jews hold that according to the Scriptures God created the world and everything in it only slightly more than 6,000 years ago. In contrast, science teaches that dinosaurs appeared on earth millions of years ago. "This is like seeping sacrilege," exclaimed Rabbi Zvi Gefner of Aguda's Religious High Court, which decides which foods get the coveted kosher label. ". . . Dinosaurs symbolize a heresy of the creation of the world because they reflect Darwinistic theories."

So heated was the controversy that CNN's television coverage showed one Orthodox Jewish rabbi scurrying by the theater in Jerusalem where *Jurassic Park* was playing shielding his eyes from the offending dinosaur posters prominently displayed outside the movie house.

Are the Bible and science really so at odds with each other that the Jews have to cut the pages out of their encyclopedias? Or so that fundamental Christians must insist, as many do, that Noah had dinosaurs on the ark? Or even that it's all a big paleontological lie, and they never existed at all?

Religious differences, of course, have been around at least since Adam and Eve's first-born son Cain slew his brother Abel because God accepted Abel's offering but rejected his.

One of the most famous modern "battles" was the Scopes Monkey trial, as it became known, fought in the Bible Belt courts of Dayton, Tennessee, July 10-21, 1925. John T. Scopes, a Dayton high school teacher, was charged with violating state law by teaching Charles Darwin's theory of evolution.

Clarence Darrow, attorney for the defendant, was a notorious agnostic. One of the most brilliant criminal attorneys ever to live, he would pretend to fall asleep and snore while the prosecution presented its case to the jury.

And in the opposite corner, William Jennings Bryan, attorney for the prosecution. Political evangelist, fundamental Christian, and three-time presidential nominee, Bryan was a magnetic and gifted debater. His admirers referred to him as the "golden-throated orator."

A British naturalist, Darwin's theory revolved around the mechanism of natural selection (survival of the fittest), acting upon heritable variation. That is, nature "selects" those animals or plants which are best able to adapt to conditions of their environment, allowing them to live longer and reproduce. Each succeeding

2

generation maintains its own individual identity due to heredity. But it also continues to evolve, or change, by adaptation to variations within its habitat, such as temperature and food supply.

So far, so good. After all, we all know that, to one degree or another, animals do adapt, or change, to fit their environment. Some grow thicker, longer coats to protect them from winter's harsh clime. Others, like the Arctic fox and grouse, experience color changes that enable them to blend against the alternating seasonal backgrounds. Bears store up enormous quantities of food in the form of fat and pass away the dark wintry days snug in their beds.

But it was not the teaching of these simple adaptations which so alarmed and infuriated the Christians of Dayton, Tennessee. What induced the frenzy which accompanied the Scopes trial was that Darwin's theory suggested that life had its beginnings billions of years ago when cells, occurring in primeval waters, eventually expanded and developed through the powers of natural selection and adaptation into organisms capable of colonizing land. It was from these early beginnings, Darwin asserted in his *Origin of Species*, that humans eventually evolved from an arboreal quadruped – an apelike creature which walked on four feet and swung from trees.

And no one was going to make a monkey out of the good citizens of Dayton! John Scopes was convicted and fined $100. But 42 years later, the law was repealed.

Yet the same fine Hand which created the universes and set them in motion also ordained and established the laws of science and nature. And it therefore follows that science and Scripture can have no significant *valid* conflict with each other.

And so, while fundamental Christians and Jews need not accept that the world as we know it today randomly evolved from a primeval, chaotic state into its present forms with all their complexities, neither do they need to turn a blind eye and a deaf ear to well-established science.

Indeed, the reality of God becomes much more apparent when you examine science and Scripture side-by-side, without bias. For then you cannot help but observe the striking fundamental similarities.

The Biblical account of the Creation has, of course, remained unaltered down through the centuries. Science, on the other hand, has continually "evolved" – almost daily adding new information gained through recent discoveries to its vast storehouses of knowledge, and then wisely revising its theories and hypotheses to fit this new data.

As already briefly mentioned, science holds that life began billions of years ago in primeval waters, when cells were formed by living organisms surrounding organic compounds. As the eons passed and the environment changed, these organisms adapted, eventually developing DNA, chromosomes and nuclei for passing on characteristics, thus expanding their powers of natural selection.

Here at the very first we find a remarkable parallel between science and Scripture. For the Genesis account of the Creation, ascribed to the Hebrew prophet Moses, also begins in a watery environment:

> 1 In the beginning God created the heavens and the earth.
> 2 The earth was without form and void, and darkness was upon the face of the deep; and the Spirit of God was moving over the face of the waters. . . .
> 20 And God said, "Let the waters bring forth swarms of living creatures, and let birds fly above the earth across the firmament of the heavens" (Gen. 1:1-2,20).

Centuries later, the Apostle Peter penned this New Testament addendum sanctioning Moses' writings: *"For they deliberately*

4

*overlook this fact, that the heavens existed long ago, and the earth
was formed out of water and through water by the word of God. . ."*
(II Peter 3:5).

Given the long history of debate between scientists and theologians, doesn't it seem striking that the two are in agreement on
this, the most ancient and basic of premises, that life had its beginnings in water? Or was it just some far-fetched fling of the imagination that led Peter and Moses, who lived thousands of years ago
and had no access to today's vast libraries of science, to state so
clearly and unequivocally that life began in water?

No, these two men of faith were only reiterating the secrets
whispered in their ears by the Master Architect of the universes.

Briefly, the six days of Creation according to Genesis were:

First day	Light
Second day	Firmament
Third day	Dry land appears; vegetation
Fourth day	Luminaries: sun, moon and stars
Fifth day	Fish and birds
Sixth day	Animals and man

If you accept a literal time frame of six days for creation (144
hours), plus the seventh day of rest (24 hours), then, like the Orthodox Jews mentioned earlier in this chapter, you not only concur
Creation took only 168 hours to complete, but also that the world
is a mere 6,000 years old.

Yet even the most prudent of Christians need not ignore the
scientific evidence that abounds to the contrary. The truth – and
the Word of God is truth – will stand up to the most intense scruti-
ny. Rather than simply adhering to what you've always been told,
read on. Accept the "challenge" of learning the whole truth and
nothing but the truth, and discover in the process that God's Word

is not only upheld, but magnified.

Obviously, "time gaps" occurred during the period we refer to as the six (or seven) days of Creation – a position which is defended by the Scriptures. To begin with, the word "day" is not only used to denote a twenty-four-hour period, but also to indicate an undetermined period of time. For example, after Chapter 1 of Genesis sets out the progression of Creation, Genesis 2:4 states: "These are *the generations* of the heavens and the earth when they were created, *In the day* that the Lord God made the earth and the heavens. . . ."

First, note that *"generations"* is in the plural form, indicating many, and thus signifying the passage of a substantial, unknown period of time far in excess of just six (or seven) days. And, since the phrase *"in the day"* refers back to *"generations,"* it therefore also denotes the passage of more than just one day – or one week, for that matter.

Secondly, although Genesis 1:3-5 says light was created on the first day, there would not have been a literal twenty-four-hour period of night and day (evening and morning) because the sun and moon had not yet been formed.

Ah, but then God had a special reason for placing "light" first!

For the initial light to dispel the darkness did not come from what was created, but from the Creator Himself. And it was with this Light the worlds began!

(See John 1:1-5.)

Centuries after the Genesis creation account, the Apostle Peter drew a parallel between the eons of Creation and the unknown, but similarly extended, period of time between the first and second advents of Christ, saying:

> 3 "First of all you must understand this, that scoffers will come in the last days. . .

6

4 and saying, "Where is the promise of his coming?' . . .

5 They deliberately ignore this fact, that by the word of God heavens existed long ago, and an earth formed out of water and by means of water,

6 through which the world that then existed was deluged with water and perished.

7 But by the same word the heavens and earth that now exist have been stored up for fire . . .

8 *But do not ignore this one fact, beloved, that with the Lord one day is as a thousand years, and a thousand years as one day"* (II Peter 3:3-8).

God did not detail all of the events encompassed within the billions of years of creation history because, as John 21:25 similarly said of the life of Christ, *all of the libraries of the world would not suffice to hold the volumes which would have had to have been written.* And men would have become even more hopelessly bogged down in minutiae and contentious strivings.

Genesis was "condensed" because God's main purpose in writing it was to reveal Himself – not the minute details of His acts in creation.

As wise old King Solomon pointed out, *the Creator "has put eternity into man's mind, yet so that he cannot find out what God has done from the beginning to the end"* Ecc. 3:11.

With the use of the word "day" in the Genesis account of Creation, **God was simply setting a precedent.**

The dynamics of the formation of earth and sea and the endless reaches of space are, of course, mind boggling. Endless theories abound; and as ongoing research and exploration bring to light new information, theories will continue to proliferate. To the end, Solomon's words – *we cannot find out what God has done from the beginning* – will prevail.

7

But, briefly, space is full of clouds of gas and dust – great swirling clouds that are 90 percent hydrogen and helium, combined with minute particles of matter (dust). Some of these clouds are as old as the universes; others were formed throughout the eons by the explosions of dying stars. Light years across (a light year is the distance light travels in one year – about 6 trillion miles), they contain some areas which are denser than others. That is, they have clumps which contain more matter within a given volume. The more matter, the greater the gravity. And the greater the gravity, the more dust is attracted to it. The fragments of matter within this primordial womb alternately grow and break apart, some eventually gaining mass through accretion. It was in this manner, science tells us, that our own solar system (including Earth) was eventually formed.

For the first 700 million years or so of its development Earth continued to gain mass from the bombardment of lesser bodies. It eventually reached a state of stability, its surface covered with "oceans" of hot rock and the spatial "flotsam and jetsam" from these collisions. Although our sun had not yet run its first course across the sky, our planet lay swathed in light from these billions of impacts and the resulting radioactive decay. Whether you believe the first light to spread its vast wings across the limitless universes emanated solely from (or was) the Creator Himself, or that it began as a result of radioactive decay, science and Scripture are nevertheless in accord: *light was there "in the beginning."*

"And God said, 'Let there be light;' and there was light" (Gen. 1:3).

Earth slowly cooled. And as a crust began to form over its molten seas, science says a steamy hot atmosphere rose from this early subterranean cauldron. Note the timely parallel of this steamy atmosphere with the *"mist"* of Genesis 2:6:

4 . . . In the day that the Lord God made the earth and the heavens,

5 when no plant of the field was yet in the earth and
no herb of the field had yet sprung up – for the Lord
God had not caused it to rain upon the earth . . .
6 *but a mist went up from the earth and watered the*
whole face of the ground. . . .

Incidentally, twice, to compound the importance and accuracy of
these Genesis verses, the Prophet Jeremiah (circa 647 B.C.) spoke
of the mist of Creation in this way (Jer. 10:12-13; 51:15,16):

12 It is he who made the earth by his power, who
established the world by his wisdom, and by his understanding stretched out the heavens.
13 When he utters his voice there is a tumult of waters
in the heavens, *and he makes the mist rise from the*
ends of the earth. . . .

Also of note is that the Genesis *"mist"* is from an obscure Hebrew root word *'ed*, which occurs only here and in Job 36:27 and
refers to water coming up from below the earth – perhaps rising under pressure from the radioactive decay beneath the newly
forming crust. In any event, as these steamy hot mists continued
to rise and cool and return to the ground as water, inexorably, the
first oceans began to develop.

The atmosphere (firmament) which gradually formed was rich
in water and carbon dioxide – though it initially lacked the oxygen
needed to support life as we know it. *Here, too, the conclusions of*
science are consistent with the progression of the Genesis timetable:

6 And God said, "Let there be a firmament in the
midst of the waters, and let it separate the waters
from the waters."

8 And God called the firmament Heaven. And here was evening and there was morning, a second day (Gen. 1:6,8).

Meteorites and comets continued to pommel our planet's surface over the eons. Slowly islands formed.

Thus, here, too, we find science and Scripture in chronological embrace as to the events *of the third day:*

9 And God said, "Let the waters under the heavens be gathered together into one place, and let the dry land appear." And it was so.
10 God called the dry land Earth, and the waters that were gathered together he called Seas. And God saw that it was good (Gen. 1:9-10).

The things which came to pass in the next three verses are also incorporated within the third day (the creation of Earth and Seas). And therefore, yes, they are detailed before mention of the appearance of the sun. However, *we know light was already in place* (Gen 1:3-5), and the possibility remains that the appearance of vegetation and the formation of the sun simply overlapped in time and development:

11 And God said, "Let the earth put forth vegetation, plants yielding seed, and fruit trees bearing fruit in which is their seed. . . ." And it was so.
12 The earth brought forth vegetation. . . . And God saw that it was good.
13 And there was evening and there was morning, a third day (Gen. 1:11-13).

The fourth day heralds the formal appearance of the heavenly luminaries.

One of the innumerable bodies thought to have struck Earth in the beginning may have been roughly half the size of our planet. One theory is that this giant impact resulted in enough material being fractured and thrown into orbit to have created a disk around our planet from which the moon eventually accrued, taking on its spherical shape over time under the power of gravitation.

As for our greater light, learned minds hypothesize Earth's sun formed over billions of years in the center of a rotating cloud of interstellar gas and dust. Spinning faster over time, this "cloud" gradually compressed, flattening the rotating material into a disk. Mass concentrated in the center of the disk, forming a sphere of gas. As new material was slowly added, the spinning and compressing increased. The temperature and pressure that eventually built up were sufficient to fuse atoms in the sphere's core. But then, a lot can happen at 27 million degrees Fahrenheit!

And so it was that –

14 . . . God said, "Let there be lights in the firmament of the heavens to separate the day from the night; . . ."
16 And God made the two great lights, the greater light to rule the day, and the lesser light to rule the night; he made the stars also. . . .
19 And there was evening and there was morning, a fourth day (Gen. 1:14,16,19).

As light and heat beamed down, photosynthesizing bacteria pumped oxygen up. At an altitude of some thirty miles or so, an ozone layer began forming that would eventually help shield early life from harmful irradiation by ultraviolet rays and permit the evolution of more complex forms of life.

Fossils of single-celled bacterial organisms first appear in sedimentary rocks approximately 3.5 billion years old. And for almost 5/6's of its history, life on earth remained uni-celled!

Finally, some 600 million years ago, multi-celled animals entered the fossil picture. In time, these initially soft-bodied creatures were followed by watery denizens with an exoskeleton – crustaceans, turtles, fishes and the like – another parallel in time and events between science and Scripture:

"And then God said, 'Let the waters bring forth swarms of living creatures, and let birds fly above the earth across the firmament. . . .' a fifth day" Gen. 1:20,23.

As a few of these early life forms progressed to the point where they were capable of exploiting land, they left the protective shield of the waters of life and clambered up onto dry ground. Some adapted and eventually spread abroad. Then about 500,000 years ago evidence of a sudden outburst of more complex organisms appeared in the fossil record and rapidly became widespread.

Once again, scientific evidence parallels the chronological scroll of life's beginnings in Genesis. For as the sixth and final day of Creation dawned—

. . . God said, "Let the earth bring forth living creatures according to their kinds: cattle and creeping things and beasts of the earth according to their kinds." And it was so. . . (Gen. 1:24).

Thus the eons raced on as life flourished under the patient eyes of God.

During the age when the early dinosaurs established themselves (165 million years or so ago), Pangaea (Gr. *"all lands"*), a single great continent believed to have dominated an even more enormous solitary sea, began drifting apart. This action was apparently as a result of the movement of the seven major and multiple minor subterranean "building plates" upon which continents "ride."

These great slabs of rigid rock, which range from forty-four to more than ninety miles thick, "float" in an underlayer of lava, drifting several inches a year over the face of this 250-mile-deep stratum of magma.

As the continents ride these tectonic plates – rifting and colliding - mountains, earthquakes, ocean trenches and volcanoes are created when lava breaks through and flows up from the cavities below. It may have been the action of these plates that not only caused the break-up of Pangaea, but which has also caused smaller continents to continue to break up and reassemble in different ways down through the eons, until at last they assumed their present shape.

On a side note here: back in 1999 scientists from Duke University completed an unprecedented underwater study of the crust of the Earth. Using a tiny submarine, they spent over three weeks exploring a canyon near the Galapagos Islands – 1,300 miles off Columbia, South America. Known as the Hess Deep, this rift reaches 9,000 feet below the sea floor.

Channels in the Hess Deep allow lava to rise, forming vertical dikes. But contrary to the orderly vertically-pointing dikes observed by a French research team two years earlier, the Duke team found areas where dikes were twisted and cracked and tipped precariously to one side, indicative of powerful forces at work under Earth's placid-appearing surface.

These and other infinitely violent underground forces will soon bring about never-dreamed-of earthquakes, landslides, volcanic eruptions and giant tsunamis – wiping out millions of people in various parts of the world in the blink of an eye.

But returning now to the age of Pangaea. . . .

No one knows why, but as the early landmasses and seas continued to break up and reshape, 75 percent of all animal species eventually became extinct.

Plankton, a primary food source of the seas, virtually disappeared, taking with it an estimated 85 – 90 percent of the watery denizens.

Whatever the causes, Earth is believed to have undergone five mass extinctions and many lesser ones. And today it is in the midst of its greatest and swiftest extinction since dinosaurs ambled off permanently into pre-history 65 million years or so ago (an event, incidentally, which fortuitously left the world wide open for the eventual unhindered spread of man). This present extinction began 11,000 to12,000 years ago. Within a thousand years, most of North America's giant mammals – including mammoths and saber-toothed cats – vanished.

So extraordinarily abrupt was their disappearance that a widely-held belief among the scientific community is that the Extinctor was God's last act in the chain of creation – man himself!

And with the advent of man (see Chapter 2), the "generations" of the heavens and the earth are now complete:

> 26 Then God said, "Let us make man in our image, after our likeness. . . ."
> 27 So God created man in his own image, in the image of God he created him; male and female he created them.

28 And God blessed them. . . .

31 And there was evening and there was morning, a sixth day (Gen. 1:26-28,31).

CHAPTER TWO

AND THEN ALONG
CAME MAN

The controversy between scientists and theologians over Earth's origins and development has fueled the primordial stew pot of evolution into a state oft-times bordering hysteria. But no addition to that brew fires the imagination and debate as do the annals of man in the history of our planet. Anthropologists glean through the layers of the millennia in search of clues which will help them make a monkey out of man (or vice-versa), while too often Christians position themselves obdurately behind a wall of false doctrine and incomplete data.

Yet scientists, in their quest for answers as to what transpired before the recorded chronicles of yesteryear began, have never deliberately attempted to undermine Biblical truths, or they would not have drawn such similar chronological conclusions regarding the order of Creation. So let's take a quick look at a minuscule portion of the available data on the fragmented origins of man — *because in the end you're going to know still more about what God has really done.*

And about who Adam really was. . . .

Without retracing our steps far enough back in time to include the first prosimians/proto-primates which roamed the forest boughs (critters that ranged in size from squirrels to domestic cats), we'll restrict our meanderings to the biological order of mammals which includes apes and monkeys, tarsiers, lemurs and humans – bringing us up roughly to 23 to 5 million years ago – the Miocene Epoch.

A good many anthropologists will generally try to convince us (and themselves) that somewhere during this period the primates which included apes diverged into lines that would eventually evolve into hominids – human-like primates. Some of the more important fossil discoveries of primates include the following:

First up, *Australopithecus africanus*, "the southern ape of Africa," 3 to 2 million years ago. The partial skeleton of a child three to four years of age was found in 1924 in the Taung cave in South Africa. It combined both human and ape-like features. Its teeth, though large by our standards, nonetheless bore a greater resemblance to ours than to apes. And although *Africanus* appeared to have walked upright, its relatively long arms and hands made it equally well-adapted for climbing.

In late 1974 another significant discovery was found in the Awash Valley of Ethiopia. AL288-1, as she was officially designated, was eventually nicknamed Lucy. This new hominid species – *Australopithecus afarensis* – was the oldest found as of that time (3.5 to 3 million years). Lucy wasn't quite four feet tall and probably weighed some sixty-five pounds. Although her brain case was slightly smaller than the Taung younster (and about one-third the size of ours), she, too, seemed to have arms and fingers adapt-

18

ed for climbing. Still, her reconstructed skeleton bore substantial similarity to ours, and she was classified in our bipedal primate family, the *Hominidae*. Remains from another 300 individuals indicate *afarensis* was around for close to a million years.

Then in the mid 1990's another team excavating near the Afar Depression in Ethiopia unearthed a skull which could – at least in their opinion – be the *missing link*, the australopithecine that gave rise to the human race. More advanced than *A. afarensis*, the newest kid on the block was dubbed *Australopithecus garhi*, meaning "surprise" in the Afar language, because they had expected a specimen with a larger braincase and smaller teeth. *A. garhi's* age was placed at 2.6 – 2.5 million years.

Not long after, an even bigger surprise fell out of the "family tree." A team exploring in Kenya, which included Meave Leakey, daughter-in-law of renowned anthropologist Louis Leakey, stumbled across the partial skull of another new genus, *Kenyanthropus platyops*, "flat-faced man of Kenya." *K. platyops* appears to date back 3.4 – 3 million years, to the time of "Lucy" - though some of the features of the partial skull are more human-like than Lucy's.

Other discoveries, while interesting – such as *Australopithecus robustus* (South Africa 1938) – are believed to be dead ends in the direct line of hominid ancestry.

Almost as though God were deliberately leading anthropologists on a tantalizingly merry chase, Mary Leakey (mentioned above) was exploring the Olduvai Gorge in Tanzania (1959-1964) when she overturned remains of what was then thought to be the earliest known member of our own genus, *Homo*. A turning point in human paleoanthropology, he was named *Homo habilis* (Latin:

"handy man") because he was believed by many to possess stone tool-making skills. Standing as tall as 4.5 feet, his brain was only half the size of ours, but he had smaller teeth and may have had the neurological equipment for speech. His appearance appears to date back 2.4 – 1.4 million years ago.

Next in the hominid labyrinth was *Homo erectus*. First discovered in 1893 by a Dutch army surgeon on the island of Java (now Indonesia), *erectus* was larger brained and fashioned more advanced tools. Particularly interesting is that sometime in his history he learned to control fire. Specimens since discovered show *erectus* was a bit of a wanderer. His habitats may have ranged across China and as far as the tropics of Africa through the years of his history (1.7 million to roughly 300,000 years ago).

Evidence of *Homo sapiens* (archaic) – the one and only living species of the genus Homo (man) – began appearing (arguably) about 400,000 years ago. Archaeologists from Tel Aviv University claim that eight teeth found in the Qesem cave 10 miles from Israel's Ben Gurion International Airport are just that – some 400,000 years old – making them among the earliest remains of homo sapiens ever discovered (www.ancient-origins.net/news-evolution-human-origins/qesem-cave-0012718). And still other fossil sites have been found in Africa, Europe and East Asia.

One overlapping species, *Homo heidelbergensis* (700,000 – 300,00), appears to have adapted to China and Europe. Evidence indicates they hunted game with wooden spears and were possibly the first to build shelters of stone and wood. *H. heidelbergensis* also controlled fire and are considered by some to be direct ancestors of the Neandertals.

Homo sapiens (Neandertal), named for the German site of discovery in 1856, appeared in the fossil record about 125,000 years ago. They combined the "Alley Oop" craggy face and heavy brow of their predecessors with a well-developed brain roughly the size of ours.

Interestingly, the eastern Neandertal types, such as the ones found in the caves of Amud and Tabun in Israel, look slightly more modern than their European counterparts. Even more interesting, this last of the hominid groups, whose physical variations from us are too slight to be of real significance, seem to have appeared thousands of years earlier in the Middle East than in Europe.

One of the oldest modern human skulls ever found was discovered in the Jebel Qafzeh Cave near (of all places) Nazareth, Israel! Thermoluminescence, a dating technique, suggested an age of 93,000 years. *If this is accurate, modern man did not "evolve" from the Neandertals, but rather the two coexisted side-by-side within roughly the same period of time – increasing the likelihood that "punctuated equilibrium" - which we will discuss momentarily – played a hand in man's development.*

In any event, Neandertals began to disappear, inexplicably and somewhat abruptly, about 35,000 years ago. And by 28,000 years ago modern humans, with facial characteristics virtually indistinguishable from our own, had replaced them everywhere.

Clothing and tools began to reflect attention to aesthetic design. And bone flutes, the earliest known musical instruments, appeared in the archaeological evidence.

One of the better-known groups of anatomically modern man was the Cro-Magnon, whose first fossils were discovered in a cave in France in 1868. They lived 10,000 to 35,000 years ago in Europe's Upper Paleolithic period. Skilled at hunting, they banded together in small groups and migrated across France, following herds of reindeer, bison and other large animals. Bits of dyed woven cloth, sculpture, cave paintings, and engravings on stone have been found in their living sites – evidence of a cultural explosion that sets Homo sapiens apart from those who came before.

But – but - in spite of the fact that science has amassed conclusive evidence that hundreds of thousands of people were alive on our planet before Adam, evolution's role remains tantalizingly elusive. The so-called "missing link" between apes and men remains just that – *missing*. Nor can science explain why some plant and animal life forms have remained unchanged for 150 million years or more, while others seem to have evolved dramatically.

One theory is that two processes are at work. In the first, evolution is gradually taking place because of changing environmental influences, mutation or other undetermined factors. In the second, long periods of evolutionary stability are *"punctuated"* by the sudden, unexplained appearances of a new genus or species, with no transitional fossil forms to account for the abrupt morphological changes. Science calls this hypothesis *"punctuated equilibrium."*

With these *two processes* in operation, the apparent inconsistencies between science and Scripture wane still further.

Remember, scientific research indicates the last of the hominid groups – anatomically modern man – appeared thousands of years earlier in the Middle East than in Europe. **And the Middle East is precisely where Scripture places Adam, the last of**

God's recorded acts of creation: *". . . And the Lord God planted a garden in Eden, in the east, and there he put the man whom he had formed"* (Gen. 2:8).

But why was Adam manifested in Genesis thousands of years *after* the first of our kind arrived in the long corridors of prehistory?

And just how old is Adam, anyway?

Here, the fundamentalists are correct. Though thousands of "modern" men and women had already appeared *in the as yet timeless tapestry of Earth's development, Adam is indeed only 6,000 years old!*

Think again on Genesis: *"Let us make man in our image, after our likeness; . . ."* (Gen. 1:26).

An "image" or "likeness" is the exact duplication of that which it reflects — the face you see staring back at you when you look into your bathroom mirror. But since *"God is spirit"* (John 4:24) — not flesh and blood — our Creator obviously was not referring to man's *physical traits.*

Rather, at this particular point in "time," God simply arbitrarily selected one man of the flesh – Adam – to be born anew of His spirit. To have an intimate, personal knowledge of and relationship with Him!

In short, Adam was God's first elect!

More than that, Adam was the first of a small but extraordinary group of men whom God would select - or elect – down through the coming centuries to carry out some unique purpose of His own. To mention just two others who were similarly called:

23

"Before I formed you in the womb I knew you." He told the youthful Jeremiah. ". . . before you were born I consecrated you; I appointed you a prophet to the nations" (Jer. 1:5).

And as the Apostle Paul similar declared, "But when he who had set me apart before I was born, and had called me through his grace, was pleased to reveal his Son to me, in order that I might preach him among the gentiles, I did not confer with flesh and blood. . ." (Gal. 1:15,16).

With Adam, the great expanse of time – or non-time – encompassed within the Genesis 1:1 phrase, "in the beginning," during which actual events passed unrecorded on Earth's chronological scroll, comes to an end.

For with Adam, God's first elect, the Scriptures at last begin to set forth a definitive timeline and history of events!

As Genesis records:

> 3 When Adam had lived *a hundred and thirty years,* he became the father of a son *in his own likeness, after his image*, and named him Seth.
> 4 The days of Adam after he became the father of Seth were *eight hundred years*. . . (Gen. 5:3-4).

Follow the biblical "Timeline" in the last chapter of this book from Adam down to the present day, and you will see that, even though our Earth had its beginnings in the millennia before the dawn of "time," the Orthodox Jews and fundamental Christians are nevertheless correct: *it will have been exactly 6,000 years from the birth of Adam to 2070 A.D. – the year of our Lord's return!*

An extraordinary truth is revealed within this framework:

Time" as we think of it did not exist before Adam was born again in the image of God because time – and indeed life itself – are meaningless without God!!!

Please – reread that. . . .

But with the spiritual rebirth of Adam, life took on meaning. And time took on dimension. Nothing would ever be the same, for man now had a *personal relationship* with his Creator!

With Adam, God's Timeline for the end of the ages now began to unfold. And to provide "a lamp unto our feet" before the ever-encroaching night, He prepared an infallible Guidebook: *His Holy Bible.*

CHAPTER THREE

WHY GOD WROTE
THE BIBLE

Look at the first few pages of any Bible, and you'll doubtless find one or more of the following: title and copyright pages, an alphabetical list of the books of the Old and New Testaments, a preface explaining how and by what authorities that particular version came to be written, guides to footnotes and abbreviations, and an introduction.

But what you won't ordinarily find (they're mentioned in only two of the twenty-four versions we own personally) are stories of the great men of other centuries who fearlessly raised their voices against the objections of the religious authorities of their day in order to translate and distribute the Scriptures to the common people. Most Christians either don't know, or have forgotten, the price men like William Tyndale paid for the religious freedom we enjoy today – but which we are very rapidly losing because of apathy and complacency.

One latter day Christian giant, Aleksandr Solzhenitsyn (1918 – 2008), a Russian Orthodox believer, understood the tenuous nature of freedom. In 1945 he was sentenced to eight years at hard labor in the Soviet Union for criticizing Stalin, General Secretary of the Communist Part of the U.S.S.R.'s Central Committee, in correspondence to a friend. Solzhenitsyn's book, *The Gulag Archipelago*, which won the Nobel Prize for literature in 1970, is an account of the physical and mental horrors of life in the Gulag – the Soviet forced labor camp system under the Communist Party. One major theme runs through the book: *evil empires do not materialize overnight. They appear gradually over time, and as often as not with the mute – if unwitting – acquiescence of a heedless and spiritually lazy people.*

A continuing thorn in the side of the Marxist government in the years following his release, Solzhenitsyn was ultimately exiled and eventually moved to the United States for a time. While here, he observed that America's excess of material wealth had brought about a dangerous complacency.

In a frank and brilliant commencement address, *"A World Split Apart,"* at Harvard University in June of 1978, *he warned of the "dangerous trend of worshiping man and his material needs" and the resulting loss of a sense of responsibility to God and society."*

And he was absolutely right! For somewhere along the way, Christians became too "comfortable" in this nation; we fell asleep and lost what others fought – and sometimes died – to obtain. We forgot it is "the way of the Cross that leads home" and settled in our easy chairs. And we followed after teachers, preachers and self-appointed prophets who – for a shilling or two – scratched our itching ears and made us feel good about ourselves.

As a result, we are perched – blinders held tenaciously in place – on the very brink of spiritual annihilation! And that is why God, foreseeing what would happen from the beginning, sent His Word

– in written and in human form – to call us back to "the good way:"

"Thus says the Lord: 'Stand by the roads, and look, and ask for the ancient paths, where the good way is; and walk in it, and find rest for your souls'" (Jer. 6:16).

The word "Bible" comes from the Greek word *"biblia"* – meaning *"books."* It originally was used by the Hebrews to designate the *Torah*, the sacred writings of Judaism (essentially the Christian Old Testament), but the Christian church eventually applied it to both the Old and the New Testaments. In the thirteenth century, the neuter plural, *"The Books"* came to be regarded as the feminine singular, *"The Book."*

No other book in history has ever attained to its magnitude. Translated in whole or in part into over 1,500 languages, God's written Word is the most widely distributed book in the world. Its influence on culture and the history of mankind is incalculable.

The earliest version of the Old Testament still in existence today was executed in the Greek language at Alexandria, Egypt in the third century before Christ. It is commonly known as the *Septuagint* because it is said to have been completed in seventy-two days. Its use gradually spread abroad. And by the time of the birth of Jesus, it was the common form in which the Old Testament Scriptures had been dispersed for nearly three centuries.

But as Greek gradually gave way to Latin in the Roman Empire, Jerome, one of the early Church Fathers (340 – 420 A.D.), produced the Vulgate – the official Latin version. In time, the Vulgate became the Bible of European Christianity.

Yet at the dawn of the fourteenth century, there was still no complete English language Bible for use by the common people of Europe. Since the Scriptures were still primarily written in Latin, they were generally reserved for scholars, lay leaders and monasteries. The general populace could not read Latin, and the Roman Catholic Church controlled what little Scripture was read or taught.

But the arrival of the *Renaissance* (Fr. Rebirth) in Italy that same century brought with it a renewed sense of value to learning. During the century that followed, students from other European nations who had come to Italy to study carried the fruits of the *Renaissance* back to Germany, France, England and Spain, where they sparked a revival in the study of Greek and Hebrew.

Bible scholars, such as Dutch-born Desiderius Erasmus (1466 – 1536), became filled with what John Wesley would later call a "holy urgency" to make the Scriptures available to the commoners, thus planting the first seeds of the (Protestant) *Reformation*. The *Reformation* was sparked by Martin Luther, a German theologian, who believed salvation was a free gift and that forgiveness of sin was by God's grace alone (justification by faith). Concerned about the Roman Catholic Church's sale of indulgences (forgiveness of sin for a price), he posted his *Ninety-Five Thesis* on the door of the Castle Church in Wittenberg inviting a debate on the matter.

But instead of a debate, Luther met with an inquisition. Refusing to recant, he was branded a heretic and excommunicated.

But Luther was popular with the people. And the German princes, partly out of religious conviction and partly out of their desire to assert independence of Roman Catholic control, helped protect Luther from the Church. Frederick the II of Saxony went so far as to assist Luther in faking his own kidnapping and secreted him away in Wartburg Castle for nearly a year, where Luther translated the Greek New Testament into German.

Other reformers sought not only to eradicate the Roman Catholic Church's abuses of power but also to bring about a stricter obedience to God's Word. At the same time, they sought to disseminate the Scriptures into the hands of those who could read. The timely invention of the printing press by Johann Gutenberg, a German goldsmith, was about to make that possible.

The first direct translation into English from the Greek and Hebrew – and the first to be printed – was the work of Oxford-educated William Tyndale. As a young man in England, he challenged the statement by a defender of the Roman Catholic Church, *"We were better to be without God's law than the Pope's!"*

Tyndale struck the table before him with clenched fist and declared, *"I defy the Pope and all his Laws! If God spare my life, ere many years I will cause a boy that driveth the plough to know more of the Scriptures than thou dost!"*

It was not an idle boast. Tyndale worked night and day translating the Scriptures into English. But when the English authorities turned against him, he fled to Germany, completing his English translation of the New Testament in 1525.

The anger of the Catholic Church quickly flared against him when the New Testaments began arriving in England secreted in barrels and bales and sacks of flour. They accused Tyndale of perverting the meaning of the Scriptures for translating the Greek word for "elder" as "elder" instead of "priest," and for translating the Greek word "repentance" as "repentance" instead of "penance." These differences were critical because the Church had priests not elders. And the Church was built on the payment of indulgences and penance to the priests and Church, and not on repentance and forgiveness from God. *By exposing these errors, Tyndale weakened the hold of the Roman Church on the people.*

The Church demanded that the New Testaments be turned in to them and destroyed, declared Tyndale a heretic, and hired spies to find him. Betrayed into their hands by a man he trusted, Tyndale - *at the Church's direction* - was tied to a stake, strangled, and set on fire on October 6, 1536. He never had the benefit of a trial. Yet his last words are said to have been, *"Lord, open the King of England's eyes!"*

And He did:

In 1603 James VI of Scotland also became James I of England. *Tyndale's dying prayer was about to be answered.*

The following year, pressured by Puritans, King James accepted a proposal to make a translation of the entire Bible, *"as consonant as can be to the original Hebrew and Greek." And in 1611 – just seven years later – the King James Version was published and subsequently became the "Authorized Version" of the English-speaking world.*

Over the passage of time, still older manuscripts and other documents on papyrus continued to be unearthed, giving translators greater understanding of the grammar, vocabulary and idioms of the Greek. Thus, other versions continued to emerge.

Today the majority of our Christian translations contain a total of sixty-six books: thirty-nine in the Old Testament and twenty-seven in the New Testament.

However, a number of the manuscripts (books) which were omitted by the Protestant Church "Fathers" were nevertheless accepted as canonical by the Church of England and the Catholic Church. And these appear in most of their editions of the Bible grouped under the title *Apocrypha* meaning, *"things that are hidden."*

One of these manuscripts, 2 Esdras, discussed later in this book, contains keys to the mysteries of the end times.

Though the Bible relates historical events, it was written to make manifest the things of the Spirit.

The book of Genesis is the "seed-plot," the foundation upon which all else rests. It has three great themes: the Creation, the Fall, and the eventual Redemption of mankind through Christ. Woven throughout each of these themes is *the crimson thread* by which we trace Jesus Christ, the only begotten son of God, the Alpha and the Omega, from the beginning of Creation to the end of all things. From everlasting to everlasting.

Moses, author of the Torah, the first five books of the bible – also called the Pentateuch or simply the Law of Moses – denoted the origin of the crimson thread when he wrote the first and best-known words of the Bible: *"In the beginning God created the heavens and the earth"* (Gen. 1:1). *For as the Scriptures make abundantly clear, Christ was there in the beginning with God, and all things were made through Him* (John 1:1-4; Col. 1:16,17).

And all through the Old Testament and on through the New –

to the last words of the Book of Revelation — we can follow the crimson shuttle to its inescapable and incontrovertible conclusion: that as surely as Adam sinned in the garden of Eden and sin entered the world through him, so also, from the beginning, God prepared a way of escape from sin and death through His Christ:

"He is the image of the invisible God, the first-born of all creation; for in him, all things were created, in heaven and on earth, visible and invisible. . . . He is before all things, and in him all things hold together. He is the head of the body, the church; he is the beginning, the first-born from the dead, that in everything he might be preeminent. For in him all the fulness of God was pleased to dwell, and through him to reconcile to himself all things, whether on earth or in heaven, making peace by the blood of his cross" (Col. 1:15-20).

This, then, is why God wrote the Bible — that we might see Jesus, and through His redemptive act of love — His death on the Cross — receive forgiveness of sin and obtain the righteousness that comes by faith.

"Now Jesus did many other signs in the presence of the disciples, which are not written in this book; but these are written that you may believe that Jesus is the Christ, the Son of God, and that believing you may have life in his name" (John 20:30,31).

CHAPTER FOUR

THE CRIMSON SHUTTLE

So it was, at the very dawn of Creation, that Scripture commenced to weave its unique portrait of Christ. For Jesus was already there when God said, *"Let there be light"* (Gen. 1:3), and the first bright rays streaked across the limitless deep.

Even as God laid the cornerstone of the earth, and *"the morning stars sang together and all the sons of God shouted for joy"* (Job 38:7), Jesus was there.

John, the beloved disciple of Jesus, penned these incomparable words, reminiscent of those in Genesis, at the start of the New Testament gospel which bears his name:

1 In the beginning was the Word, and the Word was with God, and the Word was God.

2 He was in the beginning with God;

3 all things were made through him, and without him was not anything made that was made.

4 In him was life, and the life was the light of men.

5 The light shines in the darkness, and the darkness has not overcome it (John 1:1-5).

And as Genesis continues to narrate the beginning of "time" and history and the development of God's relationship with man – and in particular the nation of Israel – we see Jesus continuously woven within this historical framework. The unceasing wickedness of men underscored the need for a Savior, and Jesus is revealed again and again in every succeeding generation, beginning with Adam.

Adam and Eve lived in the Garden of Eden. A beautiful little earthly plot of dirt and flowers and trees, somewhere "in the east."

But of far greater significance, Eden also symbolized a kingdom not of this earth, a spiritual state in which Adam and Eve abided in the presence of the Giver of Life.

Later, Jesus called it the Kingdom of God. In attempting to explain it to the religious leaders of His day, He said, *"The kingdom of God is not coming with signs to be observed; nor will they say, 'Lo, here it is!' or 'There!' For behold, the kingdom of God is in the midst of you"* (Luke 17:21).

"The kingdom of God is in the midst of you" – where it was from the very beginning. For as the story of Creation progresses, we see two unique trees take root in *the Garden of God's Presence:*

> "And out of the ground the Lord God made to grow every tree that is pleasant to the sight and good for food, **the tree of life also in the midst of the garden,** and *the tree of the knowledge of good and evil"* (Gen. 2:9).

There were many trees in Eden. But only these two were worthy of special mention. *Of every tree, including the tree of life "in the midst of the garden," the man and his wife were encouraged to eat freely – all that is, except for the tree of the knowledge of good and evil. As to it, God gave the man specific instructions:*

". . . of the tree of the knowledge of good and evil you shall not eat, for in the day that you eat of it you shall die" (Gen. 2:17).

The world with all its richness and beauty was laid at the feet of Adam and Eve. A world in which they walked and talked in *personal fellowship* with their Creator. They had only to heed one small admonition, and all this would be theirs forever: *". . . of the tree of the knowledge of good and evil you shall not eat, for in the day that you eat of it you shall die."*

One commandment, the consequences for disobedience clearly stated, the world and the glories of eternity at their fingertips – yet first Eve, deceived by the serpent, and then Adam, knowingly and willfully ate of the fruit of the forbidden tree and separated themselves from fellowship with God.

And it is here, in God's chastisement of the serpent, that we see the first direct prophecy of Christ:

> 14 The Lord God said to the serpent, "Because you have done this, cursed are you above all cattle, and above all wild animals; upon your belly you shall go, and dust you shall eat all the days of your life.
> 15 I will put enmity between you and the woman, and between your seed and her seed; he shall bruise your head, and you shall bruise his heel" (Gen. 3:14-15).

Almost four thousand years would come and go before this

prophesy would be fulfilled in the person of Jesus Christ. Born of Mary, He was the seed of woman predestined to bruise the head of Satan – that crafty perpetrator of man's Fall – by triumphing over him through the Cross.

As the crimson shuttle moves on through Genesis, we witness the expulsion of man from the garden – driven out of God's presence, *"lest he put forth his hand and take also of the tree of life, and eat, and live for ever. . ."* (Gen. 3:22).

The tree of life still stands in the presence of God, and those who believe and overcome the world and its temptations can still share in its blessings. For Jesus said, *"To him who conquers I will grant to eat of the tree of life which is in the paradise of God"* (Rev. 2:7).

But having turned away from God, Adam and his wife were no longer entitled to eat of its fruits. Through sin, spiritual death had entered the world and separated man from fellowship with His Creator. And therefore, God –

> ". . . drove out the man; and at the east of the garden of Eden he placed the cherubim, and a flaming sword which turned every way, to guard the way to the tree of life" (Gen. 3:24).

In this verse we have one of the richest profiles of Christ to be found anywhere in the Scriptures. For the Giver of Life had foreseen Adam's fall. And out of His great love for mankind He had already prepared a way back into His presence.

Surely, as Adam, burdened by sin, trudged sorrowfully out of the garden, he must have turned for one last look at what he had lost. And there at the east of the garden – in the glow of the rising sun - he saw a glorious new sight: *the cherubim and a flaming sword – each a symbol of Jesus, guardian of the way back to fellowship with God.*

Sin and death had entered the world; paradise was lost. But God's plan of Redemption was already in place, standing at the entrance to the garden – a gateway between God and man!

From the day of Adam and Eve's departure from the garden, down through the present day, the Tempter has continued his efforts to engineer the fall of every individual who has sought solace from the storms of life in the Father's house. Perverting the true words of God, Satan has consistently employed the same perfidious techniques he used to destroy the inhabitants of Eden: *the lust of the flesh, the pride of life and the desire to control one's own destiny.*

Yet we see Jesus - through whom we can conquer all the fiery darts of the Adversary. Paul spoke of this Christian warfare in his letter to the Ephesians:

"Put on the whole armor of God, that you may be able to stand against the schemes of the devil. . . . Stand therefore, having fastened on the belt of truth, and having put on the breastplate of righteousness . . . the gospel of peace . . . the shield of faith . . . the helmet of salvation and **the sword of the Spirit, which is the word of God. . .** " Eph. 6:11-17.

At the very beginning of John's end-time visions in the prophetic book of Revelation, he too speaks of this *sword* which issues from *the living Word of God:*

> "... on turning I saw seven golden lampstands, and in the midst of the lampstands *one like a son of man . . . his eyes were like a flame of fire, his feet were like burnished bronze . . . and his voice was like the roar of many waters . . . from his mouth issued a sharp two-edged sword. . ."* (Rev. 1:12-16).

From Genesis to Revelation, Jesus stands at the entranceway to Paradise, guardian of the way into His Father's presence, walking among the lampstands, keeping watch over His Church:

> **"I am the way, and the truth, and the life; no one comes to the Father, but by me"** **(John 14:6).**

As for Adam, in spite of his transgression, it was through him and his family that God would create a Name for Himself on earth. *For even though Adam was driven out of the garden, he carried with him the knowledge of God to his generation.*

In time, sons were born to Adam and Eve, first Cain and then Abel. But it is not until Eve gave birth to Seth that we again pick up the trail of the crimson thread. For Jesus would come through the lineage of this third son. And, *"To Seth also a son was born, and he called his name Enosh. At that time men began to call upon the name of the Lord"* (Gen. 4:26).

But why does Scripture say that at this particular point in time, *"men began to call upon the name of the Lord"?* After all, long before the birth of Enosh, Cain and Abel called on His Name. Genesis records they talked with Him and brought offerings to Him. Obviously, then, the men referred to here were not of Adam's family – which further establishes that other people were not only alive during Adam's time, but even before he was born.

Yet until Adam was born – or reborn – of the Spirit of God, none other of mankind had yet had a *personal relationship* with their Creator. *But with Adam, God's first elect, we also have His first witness to the world!* And therefore, by the time Adam's grandson Enosh was born, other men had gained a knowledge of God through the witness of Adam and his family; and so they, too, began to call upon the name of the Lord!

But except to record their birth and the number of years each lived, the Scriptures have little to say about Adam's grandsons and great grandsons – the forefathers of Jesus – until the birth of Noah in the tenth generation from Adam.

A thousand years had now elapsed. Only the blink of an eye in the chronicles of "time," yet the sixth chapter of Genesis records that already,

> 5 *The Lord saw that the wickedness of man was great in the earth, and that every intention of the thoughts of his heart was only evil continually.*
>
> 6 *And the Lord was sorry that he had made man on the earth, and it grieved him to his heart* (Gen. 6:5,6).

And because the earth was corrupted and filled with violence, God determined to bring a flood of waters which would destroy everything under heaven which breathed (Gen. 6:17).

Only old Noah found favor in His eyes. And thus the Lord commissioned Noah – *a herald of righteousness* (II Peter 2:5) to his generation – to build an ark of gopher wood for the saving of himself, his wife, their three sons, and their sons' wives – eight persons.

The ark, which was approximately 450 feet long and 75 feet wide, was divided into three stories totaling 45 feet in height. The Bible doesn't record the length of time the ark took to complete, but doubtless it was many years before it was ready for occupancy. No doubt, too, word of its construction spread far and wide. "Noah's folly," the people of his day probably called it, as they stood watching from the sidelines, stroking their beards and shaking their heads, laughing as God's righteous harbinger and his sons toiled on.

But finally the day came when the ark was finished. Noah and his family entered the ark, taking with them males and females of every kind of animal and bird – wild and domestic – pairs of every creature on earth in which was the breath of life. And as the rains began to fall on the earth, the Lord shut them in, and *the fountains of the great deep burst forth* (Gen. 7:11).

For forty days the flood continued, until the highest of the mountains were covered, and everything on dry land died.

Only the tiny remnant aboard the ark remained alive. The very waters which destroyed the wicked and unrepentant were a river of life for Noah and his family. Because of Noah's unfaltering faith in God, the ark was borne up on the rising waters, a refuge from the storm.

But even as the ancient world perished, Scripture provides us with a glimpse of the crimson shuttle. For Noah's passage through the waters is symbolic of our baptism into Christ, who died for our sins:

> 20 . . . *God's patience waited in the days of Noah,*
> *during the building of the ark, in which a few, that*
> *is, eight persons, were saved through water.*
> 21 *Baptism, which corresponds to this, now saves*
> *you . . . as an appeal to God for a clear conscience,*
> *through the resurrection of Jesus Christ. . .* (I Peter
> 3:20-21).

A little over a year after the flood began, Noah's family emerged from the ark, witnesses to the genesis of a new world and the faithfulness of God. After this, Noah lived another 350 years. The genealogy of his sons, Shem, Ham and Japheth – the righteous remnant left of all earth's families – is recorded in the tenth chapter of Genesis. And from these the earth was once again populated.

But it is the genealogy of Shem with which we are concerned, for it was through him and his son Arpachshad that Abraham - progenitor of the Israelites and guardian of the crimson thread in his generation – was descended.

Abraham (nee Abram) was born in Ur of the Chaldeans at the close of the 3rd Dynasty of Ur (2000 B.C.), possibly the most prosperous and literate in the history of Mesopotamia. A center of advanced culture, with libraries, schools and temples, Ur likely had a population of some 300,000. Cuneiform tablets of clay have been found relating to religion, business, medicine, law, mathematics, government, literature and the arts. And it is therefore reasonable to assume Abraham was among the well-educated.

When Abraham was a grown man, he left the land of Ur with his wife Sarai (nee Sarah), his father Terah, and his nephew Lot, and traveled northwest as far as Haran, where they lived until the death of Terah. After his death, God told Abraham to leave Haran and go to a new country which He would show him. By faith, Abraham journeyed on to Canaan. There the Lord appeared to him and made a Covenant with him to give the land to his descendants.

The years passed, and God blessed Abraham with great possessions; but Sarah remained childless. When Abraham appealed to the Lord, he was assured in a vision that not only would a son be born to them, but his descendants would be as innumerable as the stars. *"And he believed the Lord; and he reckoned it to him as righteousness"* (Gen. 15:6). Thus, when Abraham was a hundred years old and Sarah was ninety – well past the age for bearing children – they had a son and called him Isaac.

Most importantly, through faith Abraham became the father of a new spiritual race – those people of all nations and all generations who would believe God, and whose faith would also be reckoned to them as righteousness. It is these who are the true heirs of Abraham and the promises of God – not by virtue of human descent nor through the Mosaic law, but through grace and the righteousness that comes only by faith in Jesus Christ (Rom. 4:1-25).

And so it was Abraham's son Isaac, the son born of faith in God's promise, through whom the trail of the crimson thread continued.

The years passed. Isaac became the father of twins by his wife Rebekah: Esau, the first-born, and his brother Jacob. Although it was customary for the eldest son to have preeminence, the Lord told Rebekah Esau would serve his younger brother. In doing so, God arbitrarily chose to pass the crimson thread through Jacob. And as He had appeared to Abraham, God later appeared to Jacob, *renamed him Israel,* and renewed the promise He had made to his father and grandfather – that through them a nation and kings would come.

It was Judah, the son of Jacob's first wife Leah, whom God elected to carry the banner to the succeeding generation. In a real-life script worthy of one of today's soap operas, Judah's own daughter-in-law Tamar disguised herself and tricked him into sleeping with her. From that union came twin sons, Perez and Zerah. Here, God chose to bequeath to the first-born Perez the crimson standard – the lineage through which Jesus would eventually come (Gen. 38).

From Perez, the shuttle moved uneventfully on – at least insofar as Scripture relates – to his son Hezron, and from Hezron to his son Ram. Ram became the father of Amminadab, and Amminadab the father of Nahshon. Nahshon was the father of Salmon (Salma) and Salmon of Boaz – the father of Obed by Ruth, a Gentile woman for whom the eighth book of the Old Testament is named. And to Obed was born Jesse, the father of David, who would go from shepherd boy to king over Israel.

Though handsome and with beautiful eyes, David was the youngest of eight brothers, and therefore the least expected choice for king – much less the route through which the Lord's Messiah would come. *But the Christ would not come through the eldest or the strongest, but through the one who would carry His banner high by faith.*

When God sent Samuel, one of His greatest Old Testament prophets, to the house of Jesse with instructions to anoint one of his sons as the next king of Israel, Samuel did not yet know which one God had chosen. But when he saw Jesse's eldest son, the old prophet was certain this one must be the Lord's anointed.

Not so, said the Lord! *"Do not look on his appearance or on the height of his stature, because I have rejected him"* (I Sam. 16:7).

One by one, seven of Jesse's sons passed before Samuel. And one by one God rejected them.

Samuel knew he had not erred in coming to the house of Jesse, so he inquired if all of his sons were present. *Ah,* said Jesse, *all but the youngest, David. He is keeping the sheep.* And so it was that God took from among the sheep the shepherd lad who would one day be king over His people Israel.

A thousand years later, Jesus – the "son of David" – would appear and become Shepherd over a far greater flock, the scope and magnitude of which the world had never seen nor yet contemplated.

Years after David became king he had an adulterous relationship with Bathsheba, the wife of one of his soldiers.

Though David repented and God forgave him, David's first born by Bathsheba died.

But God loved Solomon, their second son, for He saw in him a man of great faith. And it was therefore Solomon whom God chose to be His standard bearer to the next generation.

Yet Solomon, as his father before him, fell short of perfection. *God's great heroes of faith are often imperfect. But they have one criterion in common: each evidences the unfaltering trust that gives birth to the righteousness that comes by faith.* Not the "faith" of an intellectual belief in God, but the unyielding faith that commits the believer to the sacrifice of self-will, in complete subjection to the will and grace of God.

And so we follow the crimson shuttle from generation to generation for another 1,000 years, all the way to Joseph and his betrothed Mary, the virgin to whom Jesus the Christ was born.

For all of the foregoing generations the Jews had waited and watched for the coming of the promised Messiah. They expected a great warrior, a champion who would lead them in battle and restore the Hebrew nation to its former glory. But instead God sent them a servant Savior who said, *"My kingdom is not of this world"* (John 18:36).

They looked for a king. But God sent them a Shepherd. And so they missed Him.

CHAPTER FIVE

BEWARE THE POWER OF SUGGESTION

It was uncomfortable and embarrassing, strapped into the elaborate lone chair perched up on the high podium in front of some of America's finest criminal lawyers. Chicago 1961.

This was a polygraph chair – the most elite lie detector equipment manufactured in the world at that time.

The event was the Northwestern University School of Law Short Course for Criminal Defense Attorneys – a sophisticated refresher course on how to make lots and lots of money by getting criminals off. I was a participant in the seminar and the volunteer guinea pig for the lie detector demonstration.

"Just settle down here in the chair, Gene. Loose your tie. That's it. Relax and take it easy while I hook you up." The polygraph instructor droned his memorized spiel, as he rigged all the dials and gauges and sensors which made up this intricate piece of catch-the-bad-guy equipment. This machine is so sensitive it can actually "record" your thoughts. By microscopically measuring your blood pressure, respiration, the electrical conductivity of your epidermis, your heart beat, body temperature, the pressure of your limbs on the arms of the chair, any movement of your fingers or

feet and such – if you even so much as *think about lyin'* – it'll catch you!

The polygraph instructor was wearing a cordless lavaliere microphone, and his every whisper boomed out across the ancient velvet-draped hall.

Then it happened!

"Uh, Gene, ah, have you had any recent cardiac events?" He almost sounded a little embarrassed to ask me as he looked in surprise at the various ink squiggles already recording on my graph.

And BINGO!

The machine went absolutely bonkers!

The tiny pens made berserk ink squiggles all over the paper! Like a bomb exploding, the machine caught my subconscious thoughts long before they reached the conscious level of my mind. It didn't catch me lying in this particular instance. It caught me subconsciously worrying about my cardiac condition.

I was the victim of the power of suggestion.

Your everyday thinking and reasoning are on what psychologists call the "conscious level," or in your "conscious mind." But simultaneously, twenty-four hours a day, every second of your life, your "subconscious" mind never stops receiving external stimuli, storing and formatting the information which it receives, and then distilling it and making qualitative judgments about it and passing its conclusions on to your conscious mind.

The polygraph examiner knew that I knew he could tell something about the condition of my heart just from all his hookups. It was a little like being connected to an EKG and an EEG simultaneously. My heart was tough as steel back in those days. But he intentionally tricked my subconscious mind into believing he had seen some sort of cardiac problem on the graph. And that made my central nervous system burst out with all kinds of responses without my conscious mind entering into the process at all.

And of course the hip audience immediately caught on and howled at my expense!

The power of suggestion!

"Nothing is so unbelievable that oratory cannot make it acceptable." Cicero said.

You ought to write these words down in the front of your Bible and highlight them in neon yellow: *Beware the power of suggestion!*

Many billions of dollars' worth of annual advertising budgets around the world testify that the power of suggestion is one of the greatest motivating forces on our planet. The ad executives subliminally suggest if you'll buy their products you'll become rich or beautiful or popular or successful – or whatever. And your subconscious mind believes them and tells your conscious mind to purchase that product. And you do! It's that easy.

So what does all this have to do with Jesus?

Very simple.

Most of the error and dissension and denominational fragmentation throughout the centuries of Christianity came from the simple power of suggestion. We all tend to be more suggestible when experiencing intense emotions, such as, for example, religion evokes. And down through the years, many Bible teachers and preachers have planted their own personal, erroneous interpretation of various Scriptures into impressionable people. And error entered. And then multiplied geometrically.

It reminds me a little of Vladimir Ulich Lenin, the charismatic hero of the Russian revolution. Ever since he died in 1924, Soviet peasants have been forming long lines, twenty-four hours a day, to trudge past his coffin in Red Square and take a look at the supposed remains of the hero of their revolution. Only it has never been proven it's really Lenin lying in state there in the glass-encased casket in the shadow of the Kremlin instead of a wax dummy. Still, millions of the "faithful" have filed by his body since the tomb opened.

I was there back in 1976, ten degrees below zero at half past midnight, with Dmitry Sinilnikoff, a Russian physicist whom I met in Leningrad.

"Dimitry, do you really think that's Lenin's body in there?" I asked my new friend, who hated his Soviet government with a vitriolic passion.

"No." He shook his head. *"But the government pretends it's Lenin, and I pretend to believe them."*

But each of us has been the victim of the power of suggestion to one degree or another. It hits the educated as well as the illiterate.

Just for example, one of the major yachting supply companies in America sells an acupuncture wrist band, which is simply an elastic bracelet with an obtrusive little plastic button fixed on the inside of the band that presses against your wrist when you wear it. And they claim it can prevent mal du mer – seasickness. And for some it will. The folks who buy these gimmicks aren't dummies; they're just victims of the power of suggestion.

Similarly, each year clinical laboratories conduct test trials of new medications. Half of the people in the trial group receive the experimental drug. The other half receive placebos containing no medication. But none of the patients know which they are being given. A few months later the tests are concluded. And, sure enough, a percentage of the folks taking the placebos will say they are feeling much better.

Psychological suggestion!

Or how about a $170 stainless and gold bracelet which is *guaranteed to promote enhanced circulation, naturally benefit sore, strained muscles and joints, stimulate the 15 acupuncture points of the wrist, reduce stress and promote overall good health.* And how, you doubtless are asking yourself, does it accomplish these miracles? *Because the six strategically arrayed, neodymium magnetic disks on the inner surface stay in constant contact with your wrist!*

According to an internet report a few years ago, marketers had sold $1.5 billion worth of magnets and related products for folks to strap on themselves in various places to cure whatever it was that ailed them. (www.healthpsych.vanderbilt.edu/HealthPsych/magnet_therapy.html)

The power of suggestion.

But if "magnet therapy" isn't your bag, and instead you'd like to lose a few pounds, one catalog we know of sells a nifty little cleansing bar that makes weight loss possible (or so they tell you) while you shave, shine, shower and shampoo. It's the incredible *"seaweed slimming soap,"* which, for a mere $18.90 a bar, *"eliminates subcutaneous fat, increases blood circulation and metabolic rate as well as breaks down fats and proteins. . . ."* You simply *"massage into the skin, the extract from the deep seaweed plant penetrates to the subcutaneous layer skin while your pores are open during a warm shower,"* and – voila! – you're on your way to a slimmer, trimmer you. (I could use some of that!)

Psychologists call it autohypnosis. Believe long enough and hard enough that you have the innate power hidden within you by which you can have anything or do anything or be anything – and you can. Many of today's preachers teach a similar "gospel." And guess what. . . . They're just about right.

Completely independently of God there is almost nothing you cannot be or have or do if you believe it and drive it into your subconscious mind strongly enough. When my brother Jim, a medical doctor, was Chief Resident at a hospital in Atlanta in the 50's, he admitted an old farmer with an inflamed appendix. When the man arrived at the hospital, he was wearing a heavy piece of copper wire around his right wrist.

"What's this thing for?" My brother asked him.

"For my rheumatiz, Doc."

"That's just superstition." Jim assured him as he removed the wire.

The old farmer said nothing. But the next morning while making his rounds my brother walked up to the patient's bed and saw that his right wrist was grossly swollen. The man never said a word. He just stared up at my brother ruefully as though to say, *"I told you so!"*

A few minutes later Jim was down in the basement of the hospital, stripping the insulation off some copper electrical wire to replace the old man's bracelet, all the while wondering to himself, *"How am I going to explain this to the Board of Regents if some-*

one catches me down here!?"

Let me give you an example of how one insignificant error has crept into and permeated the entire Christian world by the power of suggestion. Have you ever heard pastors or Bible teachers talking about the "antichrist?" The antichrist who, many say, is going to make war against the righteous in the end times? Some believed Napoleon was the Antichrist. And I have a friend who once thought Henry Kissinger might be the Antichrist. He even wrote a book about it.

Only the Bible does not anywhere state "the Antichrist" is coming in the future.

The only writer in the Bible to mention "antichrist(s)" was grand old John in 1 John 2:18,23 and 4:1-5, and II John 1:7. And "antichrist" was plural; there were a bunch of them; and they were alive when John was writing. But it's not "the antichrist" who is going to appear on the scene one day and mark his number on your forehead or hand or whatever. He is properly called the "beast" (Rev. 13).

But you hear the erroneous term so often your subconscious mind ultimately accepts it. And you find yourself believing it and repeating it.

Long before our modern day so-called faith healers came on the scene, a German born physician named Franz Anton Mesmer happened along one bright day in 1734. Mesmer claimed an invisible fluid, acting according to the laws of magnetism, emanated from the human body and permeated the universe. And this "animal magnetism," as he called it, could supposedly be activated by any magnetized object and manipulated by any trained person. Utilizing iron magnets and trance-like states folks called "mesmerism," he assured his neurotic patients he'd heal them of whatever ailed them. Mesmer's magnets and razzmatazz were just so many stage trappings, but "believers" flocked to his office in Paris. And so effective was the "good" doctor's use of the power of suggestion that many were actually healed – at least temporarily – of nervous disorders. Mesmer enjoyed a highly lucrative practice before the dubious French government ordered an international commission – which included Benjamin Franklin – to investigate.

Mesmerism was declared to be nothing more than a clever deception and declined thereafter. But a few decades later, the trance state induced by Mesmer led to the development of hypnosis.

Hypnosis – what is sometimes referred to by members of the American Medical Association as a "complementary therapy" to standard treatment – refers to a special psychological state in which an individual becomes highly responsive to extended preliminary suggestions by a trained hypnotist. Suggestions which are generally agreed upon in advance between the hypnotist and the subject. Some people respond more significantly to these suggestions than others and experience alterations in behavior and sensation.

For example, the hypnotist may suggest to a smoker he or she will never again be able to tolerate the smell or taste of cigarettes. And it happens. Or, as was the case with a personal friend of ours, the hypnotist suggested she would not feel any pain in the dentist's chair. And sure enough, she didn't. Feelings of anxiety, stress and lethargy have all been mitigated in some patients by the use of hypnotism.

It was the power of "Reverend" Jim Jones' insane suggestion

which persuaded over 900 poor wretches in Jonestown, Guyana, to feed cyanide-laced punch to their children, and then drink it themselves, back in November of 1978. (www.guyana.org/features/jonestown.html)

And it was similarly the power of suggestion that persuaded thirty-nine members of the Heaven's Gate cult to take the pipe in a mansion out in posh Rancho Santa Fe, California, almost two decades later in March of 1997. Their fearless leader, Marshall Applegate, Jr., somehow persuaded his followers it was imperative they "evacuate" Earth as soon as possible. He then convinced them the best way to do so was to commit suicide, whereupon their souls could board a space craft he claimed was following in the wake of the Hale-Bopp comet. Utter unthinkable and unspeakable insanity. Yet Applewhite and 39 members of his cult mixed up a potion of phenobarbital with applesauce or pudding, washed it down with vodka, and then placed plastic bags over their heads after ingesting the mixture to ensure asphyxiation – just in case the drugs didn't kill them! (www.culteducation.com)

These were housewives, computer gurus, ordinary people. But they shared one common denominator: they were all highly susceptible to the power of suggestion.

But then, mainline Christianity similarly suffers from human suggestibility. For example, in my experience, some ninety percent of the messages in "tongues" which are heard around the world in "full gospel" meetings are not from the Holy Spirit. They are a product of some generally well-intended person's response to prior repeated psychological suggestions. A similar proportion of the "prophesies" today are merely the result of the power of suggestion and are not from the Lord.

There are many great men and women of faith within Christianity. But religions and cults also draw suggestive, misguided people who tend to latch onto the false theologies propagated by phony "ministers of the gospel" who promise to help them fill the empty hole in their lives.

But just because a preacher or a teacher talks about a man named Jesus doesn't make them real.

Christianity is bursting at the seams with false evangelists, pastors and priests, teachers and so-called faith healers who are duping the sheep and conning them out of millions and millions of dollars, all in the name of Jesus.

How can you tell the true Christian ministers from the pious imposters? Simple. The deceivers are the ones who are always talking about finances and money and asking you to send them some of yours. *"Sow a seed out of your need!"* They coax and beguile. And many well-meaning people, duped into believing they are doing good, or that they can entreat the favor of the Lord Jesus Christ for a price, fill the coffers of these charlatans to overflowing.

You owe it to the real Jesus – with the nail scars in His hands – not to allow these false teachers and counterfeit faith healers and their orchestrated "miracle services" to woo you with their dynamically attractive power of suggestion, their palatial stage trappings, fancy clothes, makeup and diamond jewelry, and their enticing, pretty-on-the-outside but rotten-on-the-inside, holy-rollin', give-and-you'll-get-back-even-more, false, seed-faith theologies.

Wake up, Christian! Our time is nearly up. The end is almost here. And you cannot afford to be led astray. It is time to turn away from the money-changers who have exploited God's House for their own personal gain!

If you sincerely want to know what the Bible really means – what the Creator of the world has to say *to you personally* – then get alone with Him, preferably every day. *Talk to Him! And read your Bible! Over and over. Even better – get yourself a good Bible encyclopedia and really study the Word. Scripture for Scripture. And believe it! Not just the parts which are "convenient." But every word!*

As the Apostle Paul admonished Timothy, his son in the faith:

". . . All Scripture is breathed out by God and profitable for teaching, for reproof, for correction, and for training in righteousness. . ." (2 Tim. 3:16).

CHAPTER SIX

THE CAKEWALK GOSPEL

There are a lot of deadly false teachings making the rounds of mainstream churches today. Candy-coated, easy-way-to-heaven doctrines which need to be exposed for the error they are.

Jesus warned us—

> 13 "Enter by the narrow gate. For the gate is wide and the way is easy that leads to destruction, and those who enter by it are many.
> 14 For the gate is narrow and the way is hard that leads to life, and those who find it are few" (Matt. 7:13-14).

The Gospel of the Lord Jesus Christ literally cost Dietrich Bonhoeffer everything. Adolph Hitler had attempted to bring into being a Protestant church which would support his government. Bonhoeffer, a Lutheran pastor, was among the minority who stood in courageous opposition to Hitler's Nazification of the churches and persecution of the Jews. He was imprisoned in the Flossenburg concentration camp and eventually executed on April 09, 1945, not long before Hitler took his own life. But Bonhoeffer's letters and theological works not only had a wide influence on post-World War II youth in Germany, but continue to impact Christianity at large today. And he wrote, in *Nachfolge* (Discipleship), 1937:

> "Cheap grace is the preaching of forgiveness without requiring repentance. It is baptism without church discipline. It is communion and absolution without personal confession. It is grace without discipleship; grace without the cross; grace without Jesus Christ, living and incarnate. . . . Costly grace is the treasure which is hidden in the field — for the sake of which a man will gladly go and sell all he has. It is the pearl of great price for which the merchant will sell all of his other goods to buy. It is Christ, for whose sake a man will pluck out the eye which causes him to stumble. It is the call of Christ — at which the disciple leaves his nets and follows Him. . . . Such grace is costly because it calls us to follow; and it is grace because it calls us to follow Jesus. . . ."

There is no life more difficult than walking in the footsteps of Jesus!

Yet a sham, name-it-and-claim-it, prosperity propaganda to the contrary is being sold to gullible and immature Christians at an astronomical profit to the false preachers.

The oft-beaten and jailed and eventually martyred Apostle Paul said, in one of the Bible's most poignant verses, *"If for this life only we have hoped in Christ, we are of all men most to be pitied"* (I Cor. 15:19). The true Christian walk is so very difficult, it wouldn't appear to be worth the sacrifice for just this life here on earth.

But Bible truths don't bring in the big bucks. There's no market for martyrs today. Success stories and doctrines of convenience are what sell. And too many of today's preachers are willing to peddle a watered-down, sugar-coated gospel to fill their pews Sunday mornings.

Over three hundred years ago the world-renowned English mathematician and philosopher Sir Isaac Newton (1642-1727) propounded philosophical and mathematical truths that still enlighten the world today. But of far greater importance were his own unfaltering faith and unyielding devotion to the Cross of Christ. Even way back then Newton saw all the easy-way-to-heaven doctrines liberal theologians were pumping out, and he predicted: *"About the Time of the End, a body of men will be raised up who will turn their attention to the Prophecies, and insist upon their literal interpretation, in the midst of much clamor and opposition."* As Newton would be the first to tell you – were he not in a far, far better place – *it is "the Time of the End!"* And the "clamor and opposition" to the pure Word of God grow stronger every minute!

The time Paul spoke of in his letter to Timothy (2 Tim. 4:3,4) is now:

"For the time is coming when people will not endure sound teaching, but having itching ears they will accumulate for

themselves teachers to suit their own passions, and will turn away from listening to the truth and wander off into myths."

Take, for example, the relatively new and utterly erroneous pre-tribulation rapture theory. The word "rapture" doesn't even appear in the Bible. Yet folks have heard this false teaching so often that many have accepted it as "gospel truth" in spite of biblical warnings to the contrary.

In Luke 21:25-28,34-36, Jesus Himself says,

"And there will be signs in sun and moon and stars . . . distress of nations in perplexity because of the roaring of the sea and the waves. . . . For the powers of the heavens will be shaken." And then, the Lord says, *"they will see the Son of Man coming in a cloud with power and great glory. . . . Now when these things begin to take place, look up and raise your heads, because your redemption is drawing near. . . . [But] watch yourselves. . . . for it will come upon all who dwell on the face of the whole earth. . . . stay awake at all times, praying that you may have strength to escape all these things . . .*

When Jesus knew His time here on earth was nearing the end, He told His disciples He was going to be crucified (Matt. 16:21) and would be returning to the Father in heaven. But He also said that one day He would be coming back for them (John 14:2,3). And they quite naturally asked Him: *"Tell us, when will these things be, and what will be the sign of your coming and of the close of the age"* (Matt. 24:3)? Jesus' reply was another series of warnings:

Be careful that you are not led astray; . . . there will be wars and rumors of wars, famines and earth-quakes. . .; you will be delivered up to tribulation; many will be put to death; and you will be hated by all for my name's sake. And because things will be so very difficult, He told them, *many will fall away; . . . lawlessness will be increased; and the love of most people will grow cold.*

But now listen to this – *"But the one who endures to the end will be saved"* (Matt. 24:13).

Not he who endures to the rapture. *But he who endures to the end!* Luke 21:34-36 similarly sets forth what must happen before Jesus returns. And these words, too, resound with warning:

"But watch yourselves lest your hearts be weighed down with . . . cares of this life, and that day come upon you suddenly like a trap; for it will come upon all who dwell upon the face of the whole earth. But stay awake at all times, praying that you may have strength to escape all these things that are going to take place, and to stand before the Son of man."

Jesus was not speaking to those left on earth after some so-called rapture, or He would have said so, *but to all who dwell upon the face of the whole earth.*

Incidentally, the Greek word interpreted in the version above as *"strength to escape"* is alternately rendered, *"to be strong to another's detriment"* or *"to prevail against,"* by early Greek writers such as Dionysius – a judge of the Areopagus converted under the ministry of Paul (www.biblesuite.com). The phrase *"strength to escape"* was never intended to suggest, as some teach, that Christians are going to have an *escape hatch* they call the "rapture."

In a call to the saints to arm themselves, not only against the present day schemes of the devil, but also for the times to come in the battle against "the spiritual forces of evil in the heavenly places," (Eph. 6:12), the Apostle Paul wrote:

"Therefore take up the whole armor of God, that you may be able to withstand [i.e. to stand against, resist] *in the evil day,* and having done all, *to stand firm."*

The words of William Gurnall echo ever more loudly, *"this is a call to battle"* (The Christian in Complete Armour, Vol. 1, 1865). There is no thought of escape or retreat here, no hope of being taken out of the battle.

Corrie ten Boom – author of *The Hiding Place"* and other books – was one of the finest Christians to ever live. During World War II her family risked their lives to help many Jews and other fugitives escape the Nazi Holocaust. Eventually the authorities learned of their efforts, and Corrie and her father and sister were sent to horrible Nazi concentration camps. Separated from his daughters, their father died ten days later (at age 84) and was buried in an unknown grave in a paupers' cemetery.

Months later, just before Christmas, Corrie lost her beloved sister Betsie (age 59) to the inhumane conditions at the notorious Ravensbruck.

Corrie knew about "tribulation" as few others have ever known. And she was persuaded that believers are going to go through times of extraordinary hardship before the Lord returns. In her book, *Marching Orders for the End Battle* (CLC Pub. 2012) she wrote that, having gone through prison, *she felt a divine mandate to go tell the world she believed Christians were in training for the tribulation.*

Seven times Revelation quotes the Lord Jesus as saying it was **only**, *"The one who conquers and who keeps my works until the end . . ."* (Rev. 2:26) who will *"not be hurt by the second death"* Rev. 2:11); and who will be granted the right *"to eat of the tree of life which is in the paradise of God"* (Rev. 2:7); and who will *". . . sit with me on my throne, as I also conquered and sat down with my Father on his throne"* (Rev. 3:21).

Hear it again: not he who gets raptured and taken out of the fire, but *"he who conquers and keeps my works **until the end!**"*

The Apostle Paul, who suffered great things for the kingdom of heaven, encouraged saints to continue in the faith, at the same time warning them: *"It is through many tribulations we must enter the kingdom of God"* (Acts 14:22).

And throughout Revelation, the last book of the Bible, we plainly see believers – the true followers of Christ – still here on earth. Chapters 6:9-11 and 9:3,4 make specific reference to their presence.

A few chapters later, with two-thirds of the tribulation already over, the dragon (Satan) goes off to make war "on those who keep the commandments of God and bear testimony to Jesus. . ." (Rev. 12:17).

Then in Chapter 13 the two beasts arise; and those who would not worship the image of the first beast are killed (13:15).

And then, in Chapter 14, believers are admonished, **"Here is a call for the endurance of the saints, those who keep the commandments of God and their faith in Jesus. . . . Blessed are the dead who die in the Lord from now on"** (14:12-13).

Who are all these "saints" who are keeping God's commandments, bearing testimony to Jesus, refusing to worship the image of the beast, and dying in the Lord if the Church has already been raptured out of the tribulation?! Surely, you do not believe there are that many people being saved after a so-called "rapture!"

Again: *beware the doctrines of convenience!*

And here's another one: the doctrine of eternal security. *"Once saved, always saved,"* as they say. But it's not in the cards either. More importantly – it's not in the Bible. You are not eternally secure. You can turn your back on God any time you wish. Lots of folks do. Remember, twice in the same verse of Ezekiel, God explicitly warned through the prophet that, *". . . The righteousness of the righteous shall not deliver him when he transgresses . . . the righteous shall not be able to live by his righteousness when he sins"* (Eze. 33:12).

When God created the heavens and the earth, He decided in His wisdom that He wanted a small group of spiritually perfect human beings who would fellowship with Him throughout eternity (Matt. 5:48). Only Adam and Eve betrayed Him and turned the world over to that old serpent, the devil, and the deceiver has ruled it ever since (John 14:30).

But now God has given you and me a way back into His kingdom and into fellowship with Him through Jesus Christ. It's not easy – *the way is narrow and hard that leads to life* .... But if you really are ready and willing to die to self, then you can live in His kingdom with Him *today!* If you abide in Christ, and let Him live His life through you, then you have found the entranceway to the eternal Kingdom of God.

Forget the false teachers who want to lead you away from the truth – away from the narrow way that leads to life. Instead, follow in the footsteps of Jesus, *the founder and perfecter of our faith, who for the joy that was set before him endured the cross, despising the shame, and is seated at the right hand of the throne of God"* (Heb. 12:2).

CHAPTER SEVEN

THE POWER OF
THE HOLY SPIRIT

Some of the prettiest places on earth are the Hawaiian Islands. We lived there briefly many years ago. You could almost toss a pebble from our front porch into the beautiful blue Pacific.

But this particular afternoon we were in the restaurant of the luxurious Honolulu Country Club, on the island of Oahu, looking out over this tropical paradise with the ocean stretching from horizon to horizon. The occasion was a Full Gospel Businessmen's Fellowship luncheon meeting, and I was the guest speaker. There were probably 300 businessmen, some with their wives and guests present, and it had been a marvelous meeting. *God was there!*

Among the people coming forward at the altar call, asking the Lord to forgive them and to come into their heart, was a young mainland medical doctor.

"Oh, God, please forgive my sins." He knelt and prayed in a whisper with me. *"Let me start my life over. Please forgive me and come into my life. . . ."*

It is a holy moment when a soul is reborn into God's kingdom. But after a few minutes I had to move on to pray with the other people who had come forward.

Then suddenly I heard it!

The blaring of loud voices shattering the peace and joy of that once-in-a-lifetime moment. I wheeled around to see the doctor being rocked back and forth by two of the men present. One was in back of him, holding his arms in the air, rocking him and crying out in "tongues." The other was standing in front of him, helping rock him back and forth, while similarly spouting in "tongues."

The joy was gone from the now wretched young man's face. In its place there was only embarrassment and confusion. One of the two men saw me looking at them. . . .

"Gotta' get him filled with the Holy Ghost!"

But let me take you back to prison with me for a moment. . . .

It's 1972, and I'm in the Federal Prison Camp on the Eglin Air Force Base at Fort Walton Beach, Florida. I've been in prison for about a year now.

I had met the Lord in a solitary underground cell in the Federal Prison in Springfield, Missouri, the first night of my fifty-year sentence.

When I went to prison, I hadn't been to a regular church service since I was a youth, when I attended the United Methodist Church of Coral Gables, Florida. But nobody there had ever really talked to me about a *living* Lord Jesus Christ. I didn't know any born-again Christians. I didn't want to know any. I knew bank robbers and drug lords and Mafia figures. I had never read any Christian books, nor watched any Christian TV, nor listened to Christian radio. I had never heard the words "charismatic" or "the

Charismatic Movement" or "full gospel." Nor had I ever heard there were some people out there who professed – through the Spirit of God (or any spirit for that matter) – to be able to speak in "unknown tongues." And although by this time I had an intimate relationship with God, I still knew very little about Christianity and Christians.

One morning I was all alone, lying on my prison bunk. I was just filled with joy because of my new life in Christ, and I was whispering to Him and telling Him how much I loved Him and appreciated what He'd done for me.

Then, totally unexpectedly, my whispers started coming out in a different language.

I couldn't believe it! It was an incredible, indescribable miracle!

I had studied Spanish, Latin, Japanese and French, and recognized a number of other foreign languages by sound. No one could have fooled me for long with any kind of made-up language.

But this was a very real foreign language I had never heard before. I lay there, almost as though I were disassociated from what I was hearing.

Suddenly, I recalled reading the second chapter of the Book of Acts, and how they had all spoken in "unknown tongues." But like other Scriptures which I hadn't understood, I'd just sloughed it off until now. We read things in the Bible we don't understand, so we just pass over them and keep on reading. Sometimes it's all we can do.

But now Acts 2 was happening to me!

I smiled and thought, *"God loves me so much and feels so sorry for me here in this prison that He is doing for me what He did for those folks back in the second chapter of Acts! Surely if He had*

73

done this for others, I would have heard about it. It's just something special He's doing for me alone."

Later that day I wrote to an old acquaintance of mine. I had grown up with Randy and had heard he was a Christian.

"Randy, you're not going to believe this! But the same thing happened to me today that happened to the Christians in the second chapter of Acts. Have you ever heard of this happening to anyone else since the New Testament days?"

Randy's response came almost immediately.

"No, Gene, you're not the only one this has happened to since the New Testament times. It has happened to a lot of people since then. It happened to me twelve years ago, and it has happened to some of my friends. Some people refer to it as the Charismatic Movement."

Still young and naïve in Christ, I dashed off another letter to Randy asking for the address of the national headquarters of the "Charismatic Movement." I wanted to write and tell them about the wonderful miracle that had happened to me in prison.

Yes, the spiritual gift of speaking in tongues, along with the other eight gifts of the spirit, is live and real in God's true Church today. You can take that to the bank!

But a note of caution. . . .

I have spoken in "full gospel" meetings, including numerous Pentecostal churches, around the world: Assemblies of God, Church of God (Cleveland, Tennessee), independent Pentecostal churches, Church of God in Christ. I even did a Saturday morning service in "The Church of God Seventh Day Pentecost" (a Pentecostal Seventh Day Adventist church). And for a time Dorothy and I attended two charismatic Bible colleges. All in all, we must have heard a couple of hundred messages in "tongues."

But only a very, very few were truly from God.

Only a handful of them were valid.

The others were simply imitations, either from false Christians in a false spirit or from well-intentioned "do-gooders" with a message they thought their audience needed to hear – whether it was from God or not.

One Sunday morning I preached a service in a beautiful Assembly of God Church in Louisiana. You could almost reach out and touch Jesus beside you in the sanctuary that morning. And at the close of the service I invited folks to come forward to the altar if they wanted to give Him their life that day.

The organist was playing, *"Softly and tenderly Jesus is calling, calling for you and for me. . . ."*

Across the church, people were working their way down the aisles to the altar – when all of a sudden some carnal lady stood up and burst out loudly in tongues right in the middle of the altar call!

Several people who were headed toward the altar stopped dead in their tracks from the shock, turned around, and went back to their pews.

"Sit down, sister, you're out of order." I said quietly. And she did sit down. But she had shattered the peaceful spirit of Christ and destroyed the work He was doing in the lives of some of the people there that morning.

She had waited quietly through the entire service until that one moment when all eyes and ears could be turned on her – when she could glorify herself – then she had spoken out.

Anybody can speak in "tongues" — with or without the help of the Holy Spirit. A lot of cults include "tongue talking" to their advantage. But then, you don't need the help of the devil either. I had a buddy in high school (back during World War II) who could speak the best "German" you've ever heard. But it was only make believe. It just sounded like German.

But the Holy Spirit does not frighten people away. He wants the lost and hurting to come down to the altar to meet Him and talk with Jesus.

It was only a few months after the church service I just mentioned that I spoke in another AG church, and an almost identical scenario occurred. Right slap-dab in the middle of the altar call. Except this time it was a man. Once again, some of the people who were coming down to the altar turned and went back to their seats.

"Sit down, brother, you're out of order."

The true gift of speaking in tongues is not a learned language, by the way. It's not necessary for someone to "teach" you how. It's not something you pick up by repeating a few catch phrases, nor is it something you acquire because someone rocks you back and forth. It comes only from the sweet and gentle Holy Spirit. And it comes quietly and naturally, like a soft breeze sweeping down out of the cool mountains.

So who is the Holy Spirit? What does He do? And how, exactly, does He fit into God's plan of redemption for our lives?

The first Biblical reference to the Holy Spirit was in the primeval chaos Genesis refers to as *"the beginning,"* when, *"The earth was without form and void, and darkness was upon the face of the deep; and the Spirit of God was moving over the face of the waters"* (Gen. 1:2).

And as the Holy Spirit – *the Power of God* – hovered over *"the deep"* – the infinite and unthinkable reaches of space and time, the totality of the immeasurable universes – Almighty God spoke into being the things that are out of the things that do not exist: *"By the word of the Lord the heavens were made, and by the breath of his mouth all their host"* (Psa. 33:6).

The embryonic waters of the deep now had a face. And oh! what a face it was: *"The heavens are telling the glory of God; and the firmament proclaims His handiwork"* (Psa. 19.1).

Yet the creation of the heavens and the earth might have been little more than an extended exercise of God's wisdom and power except for one thing – Adam and Eve.

Fashioned of the dust, in time Adam and Eve were reborn of the Spirit – the very breath of the Almighty – and were transformed by His power into His "image and likeness."

Now life had meaning!

But Eve ate of the forbidden fruit from the tree of the knowledge of good and evil and gave some to Adam, and he, too, ate.

And sin entered the world.

Eventually all mankind would be called upon to give an accounting before the judgment seat of God.

They would need an advocate!

Many of the prophecies of the Old Testament seers were designed to point a messianic finger to that Advocate who was to come – Jesus Christ. One of the best-known examples is found in Isaiah: *"Therefore the Lord himself shall give you a sign. Behold, the virgin shall conceive and bear a son, and shall call his name Immanuel"* (Isa. 7:14).

"Immanuel" – *God is with us* – in the person of the Lord Jesus Christ. It was He who would usher in "the age of the Spirit" in which all true believers would be endowed with the Holy Spirit. And it was through the power of His indwelling that mankind would come to have a new, more personal relationship with God.

In the last two verses of the Old Testament God foretold of John, the New Testament prophet who would one day come *in the spirit and power of the long-departed Elijah* (Luke 1:17) and herald the appearance of the Lord Jesus: *"Behold, I will send you Elijah the prophet before the great and awesome day of the Lord comes"* (Mal. 4:5,6).

And so it was. Four hundred years after the curtain had fallen on the Old Testament, Matthew (the first book of the Christian New Testament) opens with the genealogy and birth of Jesus Christ, then switches immediately to the advent and ministry of John:

> 1 *In those days John the Baptist came preaching in the wilderness of Judea,*
> 2 *"Repent, for the kingdom of heaven is at hand."*
> 3 *For this is he who was spoken of by the prophet Isaiah when he said, 'Prepare the way of the Lord; make his paths straight'"* (Matt. 3:1-3).

John was the messenger sent to prepare the people of his day for the imminent appearance of the Messiah:

". . . After me comes he who is mightier than I, the strap of whose sandals I am not worthy to stoop down and untie. I have baptized you with water, but he will baptize you with the Holy Spirit" (Mark1:7,8).

Not long afterward, Jesus came from Galilee to the Jordan where John was baptizing and was Himself baptized. John testified that he saw the Holy Spirit descending upon Jesus out of Heaven in the form of a dove (Matt. 3:13-17).

In this, as in all things, Jesus set the pattern for our lives. Baptism is the outward evidence of the inward change that occurs in the human heart with the putting off of self and the commitment of one's life to the will of God – something which can only take place by the power of the Holy Spirit abiding within the believer:

"And Jesus, full of the Holy Spirit, returned from the Jordan, and was led by the Spirit in the wilderness for forty days, being tempted by the devil. . ." (Luke 4:1,2).

Can we expect the same testing and temptations Jesus endured? Bet on it! Because the same enemy who got Adam and Eve bounced out of the Garden - and who immediately met and tempted Jesus at the beginning of His ministry – will likewise seek out *your* greatest weaknesses and do everything in his power to snatch you away from the Kingdom of God and from the peace and joy and love that are found in Christ. *It is only by the power of the Holy*

Spirit within us that we are able to withstand the temptations of sin and the trials that come to all believers.

John, in his matchless discourse on Christ, proclaimed, *"to all who received him, who believed in his name, he gave power to become children of God; who were born, not of blood nor of the will of the flesh nor of the will of man, but of God"* (John 1:12,13).

Hear it again – *this "power" is the abiding presence of the Holy Spirit within the believer.* It is the Power that descended upon Jesus in the form of a dove at His baptism; it is the Power that was with Him during His temptation by Satan in the wilderness; it is the Power which remained with Him throughout the three years of His ministry among men; and it is the Power by which He was resurrected from the dead.

In brief, the Holy Spirit is the Power of God in action, the evidence of His Presence.

Just before His return to the Father, Jesus said to His disciples, *Stay in Jerusalem! Wait for the promise of my Father! John baptized you with water; but you shall be baptized with the Holy Spirit. You shall receive power when the Spirit has come upon you, and you shall be my witnesses to the end of the earth* (Acts 1:4,5,8).

Think about it! For three years the disciples had walked and talked with Jesus *personally*! They had seen Him heal the sick and drive out demons and even raise the dead. And they had watched Him die. More than that, they had talked with Him face-to-face after He was resurrected! Yet, unbelievably, they were still unprepared for the difficult work that lay ahead. Thus, the Lord's parting admonition:

Wait! You are not yet ready. But I am sending you another teacher, counselor, comforter and guide – the Holy Spirit. And He will provide the strength and wisdom you will need.

Man is different from the animal phylum only because he was created to have communion with God. To be indwelt by the Holy Spirit. Not only to be known by God, *but so that we might also know Him – personally.*

And so the disciples waited. For fifty days after Passover they stayed in Jerusalem. And then—

1 *When the day of Pentecost had come, they were all together in one place.*

2 *And suddenly a sound came from heaven like the rush of a mighty wind, and it filled all the house where they were sitting.*

3 *And there appeared to them tongues as of fire, distributed and resting on each of them.*

4 *And they were all filled with the Holy Spirit and began to speak in other tongues, as the Spirit gave them utterance.*

5 *Now there were dwelling in Jerusalem Jews, devout men from every nation under heaven.*

6 *And . . . each one heard them speaking in his own language. . . .*

12 *And all were amazed and perplexed. . . .*

14 *But Peter, standing with the eleven, lifted up his voice and addressed them. . . .*

16 *". . . this is what was spoken by the prophet Joel:*
17 *'And in the last days it shall be, God declares,*
that I will pour out my Spirit upon all flesh, and
your sons and your daughters shall prophesy. . .'
(Acts 2:1-6,12,14,16,17).

Less than eight weeks earlier the disciples had all run away when Jesus was arrested. Three times Peter had even vehemently denied he knew Him. In mute fear and trembling, they had let Him be crucified. But with the coming of the Holy Spirit, they were transformed in a moment of time into men of infinite faith and courage.

So significant was the change that immediately thereafter, under the empowering of the Spirit now within him, Peter stood up before a great public assembly and boldly proclaimed Jesus as the resurrected and long-awaited Messiah. That day in Jerusalem, when the power of the Holy Spirit came on a handful of believers, the Christian Church was born. Three thousand people were added to the 120 who were assembled together when the Power of God first descended; and through His force within them they were at last prepared for the evangelistic mission to which they were called.

Within a few short decades the gospel message would be carried across the Roman Empire. And in every generation since, men and women imbued with the Holy Spirit have continued to perpetuate *"all that Jesus began to do and teach"* (Acts 1:1).

Yet the fulfilling of the Great Commission *through us* is secondary to the more personal aspect of the Spirit's work *within us.* For without the illumination of the Spirit, our ability to truly know Him is limited at best. We see *His Works* (acts), but we have no understanding of *His ways.* As the Psalmist said, *"He made known his ways to Moses, his acts to the people of Israel"* (Psa. 103:7).

For forty years the people of Israel wandered in the wilderness between Egypt and the Promised Land because of their lack of faith. And for all those years, they watched God perform great and miraculous works on their behalf. They walked over on dry land when He parted the Red Sea before them; they drank water which sprang from a rock; and they ate the food of angels which He daily provided from Heaven. Yet, though they saw all these works, *and believed He existed,* they never understood His ways.

Except for Moses.

For the wisdom to understand the ways of God is imparted only to the man or woman in whom His Spirit dwells.

Think of it like this: there is a world of difference between simply believing an airplane is capable of flying and actually being able to get it off the ground and keep it in the air. Just knowing its capabilities won't get you airborne. But understanding how it works makes you soar, up where the horizon goes on forever.

In the same way, when the Holy Spirit comes and makes His home within us, all things become possible. *The very breath of God – His power – inhabits us.* And through His power our new spiritual horizons are unlimited. He enables us to put off our old sinful nature – with the weaknesses of the flesh – and be transformed by the renewing of our minds into a new creation, righteous and holy.

Through the Spirit we have the power to prevail over sin and the vagaries of life and to enjoy the fruit that results: *love, joy, peace, patience, kindness, goodness, faithfulness, gentleness and self-control* (Gal. 5:22,23).

But as the fruit is given that our life in Christ may be enjoyed to the fullest, so the gifts of the Spirit are divided among believers for the guidance and building up of the Church:

> 1 *Now concerning the spiritual gifts, brethren, I do not want you to be uninformed.* . . .
>
> 8 *To one is given through the Spirit the utterance of wisdom, and to another the utterance of knowledge.* . . .
>
> 9 *to another faith by the same Spirit, to another gifts of healing.* . .
>
> 10 *to another the working of miracles, to another prophecy, to another the ability to distinguish between spirits, to another various kinds of tongues, to another the interpretation of tongues.*
>
> 11 *All these are inspired by one and the same Spirit, who apportions to each one individually as he wills* (I Cor. 12:1,8-11).

Most of the gifts are self-explanatory. Where confusion arises, it ordinarily does so over prophecy or tongues.

In brief, prophecy is a predictive utterance inspired by the Holy Spirit for the encouragement, consolation and maturing of the Church.

Tongues, on the other hand, are a sign of the coming of the Holy Spirit upon a believer, or for prayer (I Cor. 14:2,4,28). They can also be given – if an interpreter is present – for the edification of the Church, or serve as a sign to unbelievers if any are present (I Cor. 14:5-23).

And while the choice is yours whether to restrain, limit or even refuse any of the gifts of God, to whatever extent you do so, you simultaneously limit and restrict the working of the Holy Spirit and His power within you.

By the way, there is an oft-repeated teaching in some Christian circles that receiving the Holy Spirit is not only concurrent with repentance and water baptism – it is automatic. But this is not usually the case.

For example: not long after the Holy Spirit initially descended on the 120 believers in Jerusalem, a persecution arose against the Church, and they were all scattered through the regions of Judea and Samaria, except for the apostles (Acts 8:1). Philip, a disciple and evangelist, was one of those who went down to a city of Samaria. Many of the people there believed as he preached and were baptized (Acts 8:12).

But . . . but . . . when the apostles at Jerusalem heard Samaria had received the Word of God, they sent Peter and John down to pray for them to receive the Holy Spirit, for the Spirit had not yet fallen on any of them. These new believers had only been baptized in the name of the Lord Jesus. And Peter and John laid their hands on them, and they received the Holy Spirit (Acts 8:15-17).

Though there are biblical instances when the Holy Spirit fell on hearers and they spoke in tongues even as the gospel was being preached, the preponderance of scriptural evidence demonstrates that receiving the Spirit is not automatic; *it requires the active appropriation of a repentant and willing believer.*

The Power is His, but the choice is yours.

In other words, you must not only believe and confess your sins, but also surrender self-control of your life to the will of God without any reservation. This emptying of self is like taking out the old furniture in your house to make room for new. Get rid of the excess "baggage" you are carrying around – anything that holds you back or pulls you down and keeps you from running the race for the high calling of God in Christ:

> 1 *... let us also lay aside every weight and sin which clings so closely, and let us run with endurance the race that is set before us,*
> 2 *looking to Jesus ... who for the joy that was set before him endured the cross, despising the shame, and is seated at the right hand of the throne of God* (Heb. 12:1,2).

Put aside self, and God and His Son will come to you, through the indwelling of the Holy Spirit, and make their home with you – bringing with them all new furnishings – a new heart, a new mind, a new life, and all the fruit of the Spirit.

CHAPTER 8

"CHRISTIAN" HOMOSEXUALS: THE BIBLICAL PERSPECTIVE

Many years go someone told us the story of a missionary who landed his small bush plane near an extremely remote jungle village. Later, as he told the villagers and elders about Jesus, he held up his Bible. When he finished speaking, the old chief nodded thoughtfully and said, *"I know what you have said is true because our ancestors had that book, but they fell asleep and lost it."*

They fell asleep and lost it!

And that is just what America has done!

We have fallen asleep and lost the God of our Fathers.

Do you happen to know what the *first legal document* was that lawfully organized this Republic which we have come to call the United States of America? Ask most folks, and they'd probably guess the Declaration of Independence. Or perhaps the Constitution. But of course they would be wrong.

This nation was lawfully begun by the writing and signing of a document in the cabin of a square-rigged sailing vessel poetically called the "Mayflower," lying at anchor "at Cap-Codd," on November 11, 1620, under our "Old Style" calendar.

Forty-one of the brand new Americans on board signed it and called it the *Mayflower Compact.*

What do you suppose these men so emphatically stated was the purpose of the *Compact?* What motive compelled them, as they wrote, to *"brave the tempests of the vast and furious ocean and the terrors lurking in the American wilderness"* – tempests and terrors so great that only a few more than half of them survived the long voyage and the first year in their new country? What force was so great or cause so noble these northern Europeans were literally willing to die for it? They did it, as they so poignantly wrote, for the glory of God and to advance the Christian faith! *The Christian faith. . . .*

> *". . . We, whose names are underwritten . . . by the*
> *Grace of God. . . . Having undertaken for the glory*
> *of God and advancement of the Christian faith . . .*
> *a voyage to plant the first colony in the Northern*
> *parts of Virginia, do by these presents solemnly and*
> *mutually, in the presence of God, and one of anoth-*
> *er, covenant, and combine ourselves together into a*
> *civill body politike . . . for the general good of the*
> *colonie. . . ."*

There were ninety-eight men and women aboard the Mayflower. One was born on the voyage; four joined them from another ship. Forty-one men signed the "Compact." There were twelve other men, twenty-two women, twenty boys and eight girls in the company. In December, six died; in January, eight died; in

88

February, seventeen; in March, thirteen; leaving forty-four who are believed to have survived and to have left descendants.

But today it is illegal to "advance the Christian faith" in the schools of this nation. Non-Christians and do-gooders have desecrated the Mayflower Compact, dishonored those who died to establish "the land of the free and the home of the brave," and polluted the pure Christian standards of morality upon which this nation was founded.

America went to sleep and lost what she had gained at such high cost.

She began to doze off about the time Franklin and Eleanor Roosevelt rolled into the White House on the votes of unthinking and misguided Americans. Until then, this nation had been the most highly moral, the most evangelical Christian, and the most affluent, powerful and respected nation in history. *God had indeed gloriously shed His grace on us – "from sea to shining sea!"*

You could take a dollar bill to your bank and get a dollar's worth of gold for it.

You and your wife could walk the street of almost any city in America at night without a care.

Children prayed in classrooms across America each morning. And said the Pledge of Allegiance to the flag of our country.

Folks went to church on Sundays. Spent most of the day there, what with all the singin' and picnic' on the grounds and such. It was the best day of the week - with no dirty movies or foolish TV shows in between.

Speaking of which – allow me to digress for just a moment and ask, *Do you spend even half as much time each day with the Lord as you do in front of your TV set? Or surfing the internet?*

"Uh-Oh! Now you've done quit preachin' and gone to med-dlin'!" You say.

Pornography, adultery, fornication, obscene gestures, filthy language and homosexuality – until just a few years ago the Law very properly referred to the latter as "the abominable and detestable crime against nature" – were prosecuted in the courts regularly. And violators of reasonable standards of human conduct and common decency went to jail.

Back in those by-gone days, Christmas was Jesus' birthday. Newspapers and radios talked about *Him*. Christian carolers walked house-to-house, singing out the good news of Christ come to earth. It was a joyous time of national celebration.

And Easter was the day He arose from the tomb. Everybody talked about it and gave thanks to Almighty God. Today, it's all about bunny rabbits and Easter egg hunts.

America "went to sleep and lost it."

The people who founded this once great nation – the hard-working, motivated, intelligent, sexually-moral Christians – started becoming an impotent minority in this land. And the hand which grabbed the throttle was a lazy, ignorant, opportunistic, immoral, atheistic one. A hand that betrayed the forty-one honorable men who signed the Mayflower Compact.

Ah, but the new, unthinking herd had a solution!

These liberals had an answer!

They – including millions of complacent churchgoers – subconsciously had a God-induced "feeling" they were doing wrong. So they created for themselves a brand new "do-gooder society."

A rationalization religion. "Situational ethics," philosophers call it. Something to make them feel better about their wrong doing.

"Oh, just see how good we are!"

"We just love everybody!"

"God just loves everybody!"

A new, comfortable, feel-good-about-yourself, psychological ethical hedonistic society was born in America and quickly spread into most of the churches and seminaries and Bible colleges across this nation.

If it feels good, do it. Just don't hurt anybody else's feelings. Live and let live!

In colonial America, men and women who committed "the abominable and detestable crime against nature" could be sentenced to the death penalty, as Almighty God commanded.

Back in the Old Testament, the Creator of both male and female absolutely and forever decreed that, *"If a man lies with a male as with a woman, both of them have committed an abomination; they shall surely be put to death, their blood is upon them"* (Lev. 20:13).

How can you say that, you ask? Some homosexuals seem so kind and sweet.

I didn't say it. God said it!

One day back in 1973, while I was in the Eglin Federal Prison, one of the guards came up to me and started talking about how immoral our nation had become. During the course of the conversation, he joked, *"Pretty soon, God is either going to have to destroy America or apologize to Sodom and Gomorrah!"*

The biblical cities of Sodom and Gomorrah were utterly destroyed because the men of those two cities were engaged in gross deviant sexual behavior – particularly homosexuality. And because of their perverted carnal appetites, God rained fire and brimstone down on them (Gen. 19:24-28).

Now you would think the fiery example of Sodom and Gomorrah would have been amble warning to future generations. Yet down through the centuries, the world continued to hone sexual immorality to an extent never even contemplated by those two sister-cities. Today, even the Apostle Paul's strict admonitions in the book of Romans – which eliminate all doubt as to God's position on the matter – are mocked or ignored:

18 For the wrath of God is revealed from heaven against all ungodliness and wickedness of men who by their wickedness suppress the truth. . . .

20 Ever since the creation of the world his invisible nature, namely, his eternal power and deity, has been clearly perceived in the things that have been made. So they are without excuse;

21 for although they knew God they did not honor him as God or give thanks to him, but they became futile in their thinking and their senseless minds were darkened.

22 Claiming to be wise, they became fools. . . .

26 *For this reason God gave them up to dishonorable passions. Their women exchanged natural relations for unnatural,*

27 *and the men likewise gave up natural relations with women and were consumed with passion for*

one another, men committing shameless acts with men and receiving in their own persons the due penalty for their error.

28 And since they did not see fit to acknowledge God, God gave them up to a base mind and to improper conduct. . . .

32 Though they know God's decree that those who do such things deserve to die, they not only do them but approve those who practice them (Rom. 1:1820-22,26-28,32).

And did you catch that: God condemns even those who "approve" those who practice sexual immorality. Yet today, men and women not only commit *shameless acts* with members of their own sex, but America (and much of the rest of the world) actually embraces the people who do such things – and in many instances even honors them! Homosexuals reign on television and at the movie theater; they are idolized in sports, music and the arts. They are appointed and elected to some of the highest political offices in this nation.

Worst of all, in arrogant contempt of the Holy Scriptures, they make a public mockery of the Bible by occupying – with the churches' blessings – even the pulpits of this country!

Standing in God's house, *". . . they proclaim their sin like Sodom; they do not hide it"* (Isa. 3:9).

And the congregations of America dare to sit listlessly in their pews and allow it to be so!

No wonder the Bible warns, *judgment begins at the household of God. . . (I Peter 4:17).*

As a young Public Defender in Miami, I remember hearing one of the Criminal Court judges sentencing a homosexual who got caught for the umpteenth time plying his pastime in the men's room of the downtown bus station.

"Two years in state prison!" The judge rapped his gavel, and then muttered mirthlessly, *"It's just like sendin' a kid to a candy factory!"*

But by the 80's, the do-gooders had decided imprisonment was too severe a punishment.

And today, in an insane and sardonic twist, the moral people have been made to look like the immoral. And the amoral have become the good guys.

"Gay" rights proponents proliferate across the nation; ages-old crosses and the Ten Commandments are removed from public property; rioting is common for whatever "cause" is popular; some of America's high schools are distributing free condoms; and city/state governments provide hypodermic syringes to narcotics addicts.

But it's illegal to pray or to read the teachings of Jesus in our schools!

In the case of Santa Fe School District vs. Doe (June 19, 2000), a high school student council chaplain delivered a prayer over the intercom before varsity football games. But the United States Supreme Court ruled this practice violated the establishment of the First Amendment. And it was just the beginning of many such cases.

Parades across America "celebrate" homosexuality and lesbianism – some joined by "Christian" churches.

But true Bible-believing Christians do not renounce the Holy Scriptures nor glorify Satan by defending the behavior of non-believers.

The churches were our last line of defense, but they went to sleep on their watch, and we lost America.

Years ago, in direct disregard for Holy Scripture, the Episcopalians ordained a woman who was an homosexual. *Think about it!* Sunday morning rolls around; she gets out of bed and dresses herself in priestly garments. Then she climbs brazenly up into the pulpit and preaches *the living Word,* while personally living in direct violation of, and contempt for, *the written Word of a Holy God!* And the unthinking congregation allows her to do so.

But the same types of sexual error have crept into most of the other mainline churches, including the Presbyterian, Lutheran and the United Church of Christ.

Take, for example, the Lutherans. In 2010 the 4.6 million member denomination voted to allow *noncelibate* gay ministers *"in committed relationships"* to serve in the church. Not one, but seven, openly gay pastors were welcomed into the fold at a ceremony held in July of that year.

Less than a year later the Presbyterians made similar headlines when they, too, opened the doors to gays and removed the celibacy requirement for unmarried clergy. Fox News carried an article quoting one of the women elders at St. Mark's Tucson Presbyterian Church as exulting, *"It's a thrilling day!"* (Pub. May 10, 2011, Tara Bannow AP Presbyterian clear way for gay clergy)

Unbelievable! The Bible was struck down; homosexuality was welcomed with open arms into the pulpit of the Holy Place; and a female elder of the church calls it "thrilling!"

They substitute a gospel of oneness for righteousness; reconciliation for holiness; a live-and-let-live false spirituality for Truth; *and a do-gooder mentality for faith and obedience to the Holy Scriptures of Almighty God!*

The great Old Testament prophet Isaiah – who was martyred for his faith – warned of people like these (Isa. 5:20,21):

> 20 *Woe to those who call evil good and good evil, who put darkness for light and light for darkness. . . .*
> 21 *Woe to those who are wise in their own eyes, and shrewd in their own sight!*

Oh, but God hates sin but loves the sinner! Do-gooders chime in false spiritual benevolence. Only that statement doesn't appear anywhere in the Bible.

Then there's the Roman Catholic Church which, according to some estimates, has spent nearly 4 billion dollars settling claims and litigating lawsuits brought by victims of sexual abuse by pedophile priests within the highest ranks of the church. https://www.ncronline.org/news/accountability/ncr-research-costs-sex-abuse-crisis-us-church-underestimated (Headline 11/2/15)

Several years ago, while we were on a speaking tour of prisons and churches in Greece, I spoke in a prison in the old city of Corinth. The prison walls looked ancient enough to have been around since the days when the Apostle Paul walked the streets of the city. Back in those days, Corinth was one of the Roman

Empire's busiest centers of trade. But so utterly amoral were its citizens that "to corinthianize" came to mean to live an immoral life. Needless to say, there were a lot of problems in the church at Corinth, not the least of which was sexual immorality. I and II Corinthians were letters Paul wrote to the Christians there, probably from Ephesus, three or four years after leaving Corinth.

Never one to beat around the bush, the apostle wrote in no uncertain terms of the church's arrogant disregard of the sexual depravity in their midst. He told them the immorality of people outside the church (unbelievers) was not their concern, *but he strictly instructed them to make moral judgments of people within the church, and to reject – and eject – the sexually immoral from among their ranks!*

9 I wrote to you in my letter not to associate with sexually immoral people—

10 not at all meaning the sexually immoral of this world, or the greedy or swindlers, or idolaters, since then you would need to go out of the world.

11 But now I am writing to you not to associate with anyone who bears the name of brother if he is guilty of sexual immorality or greed, or is an idolater, reviler, drunkard, or swindler – not even to eat with such a one.

12 For what have I to do with judging outsiders? Is it not those inside the church whom you are to judge?

13 God judges those outside. "Purge the evil person

from among you" (I Cor. 5:9-12).

As though that were insufficient instruction, the apostle went on to say:

> *"Or do you not know that the unrighteous will not inherit the kingdom of God? Do not be deceived: neither the sexually immoral . . . nor men who practice homosexuality . . . will inherit the kingdom of God"* (I Cor. 6:9,10).

How could God have written it more clearly?

a. You have an obligation to judge people within the church who claim they are Christians (I Cor. 5:12);
b. If they indulge in unnatural sexual relations (men with men or women with women), you, as a Christian, are to "purge the evil person(s) from among you."

And, incidentally, Jude – the last book before Revelation – says, *". . . Sodom and Gomorrah and the surrounding cities, which likewise indulged in sexual immorality and pursued unnatural desire, serve as an example by undergoing a punishment of eternal fire"* (Jude 1:7).

One thing we have learned: ***Almighty God, the Ancient of Days, the King of kings, does not compromise. Ever. Nor will He tolerate your compromise.***

There are no true, Bible-believing Christians who approve –

or even quietly tolerate – those in their midst who practice such abominations.

To pretend otherwise is to reject the Word of God and add to the insanity that is raging across America.

SEE APPENDIX

The subject of the treatise is solemn: A War between the Saint and Satan. And that so bloody a one, that the cruellest war which ever was fought by men, will be found but sport and child's play compared to this. Alas, what is the killing of bodies to the destroying of souls? . . . It is a spiritual War you shall read of, and that not a history of what was fought many ages past and is now over; but of what is now going on, the tragedy is at present with us. And not at the farthest end of the world, but what concerns you and everyone who reads of it. The stage whereon this war is fought is every man's own soul. There is no neuter in this War. The whole world is engaged in the quarrel, either for God against Satan, or for Satan against God.

William Gurnall
(1616 – 1679)
The Christian in Complete Armour

THIS IS ARMAGED'DON

CHAPTER NINE

ARMAGED'DON
THE WRATH OF GOD

Some one hundred and fifty years ago, the great scientific minds of the era gathered for a symposium in Paris, France. During the course of that conference, a respected French scientist by the name of Pierre Berchelt stood up and declared, *"Within one hundred years . . . man will have discovered the secret of the atom. And when he does, God is going to come down with His big ring of keys and say, 'Gentlemen, it is closing time!'"*

That time is at hand.

The key is already in the lock.

The Four Horsemen of the Apocalypse, spoken of in the Revelation of Jesus Christ to St. John the Divine, have already begun a journey across this broad Earth from which there is no return. And no escape. A world formed out of chaos is being returned to the forge and to the red-hot pyres of the Great Tribulation.

Revelation, the last book of the Christian Bible, is the record of a series of visions given to John (Rev. 1:1,2) while he was in exile on the Aegean island of Patmos, fifteen miles off the west coast of Ephesus, because of his testimony of Jesus (Rev. 1:9). It relates virtually exclusively to the period of time the Bible alternately refers to as *the great tribulation, the day of the Lord, or the wrath of God.*

Revelation has been described in many and various ways. Theologians have tried to explain it in grand-sounding approaches such as dispensational, moderate futurist, spiritually symbolic, preterist (to be interpreted in its own historical setting), or historical (in terms of the history of the Church).

But John simply called it a "prophecy" of what must soon take place (Rev. 1:1,3).

In point of fact, Revelation was the culmination of many end-time prophecies, or revelations, which began in the Book of Genesis. Old Testament prophets from Abraham to Malachi, and many of those in the New Testament, foresaw these cataclysmic events approaching and warned of the times which beset us at this very hour. The great and mighty Old Testament Prophet Isaiah – whom tradition holds to be the martyr of the Book of Hebrews who was sawn in two for his faith (Heb. 11:37) – was one of those who forewarned and exhorted believers concerning the impending judgment:

> 20 *Come, my people, enter your chambers, and shut your doors behind you; hide yourselves for a little while until the wrath is past.*
> 21 *For behold, the LORD is coming forth out of his place to punish the inhabitants of the earth for their iniquity, and the earth will disclose the blood shed upon her and will no more cover her slain* (Isa. 26:20,21).

1 *In that day the LORD with his hard and great and strong sword will punish Leviathan, the fleeing serpent, Leviathan the twisting serpent, and he will slay the dragon that is in the sea* (Isa. 27:1).

In the verse above, *Leviathan* and *serpent* are metaphors for Satan – who is the embodiment of evil and chaos in today's world. But in this same verse, *"the dragon in the sea"* refers to one who is yet to come: *the first beast of the Book of Revelation - the counterfeit Christ and progeny of his father Satan.*

Conversely, it is Satan who is referred to as "the dragon" in the following verse in Revelation. About these two, John says:

> *"And I saw a beast rising out of the sea . . . a blasphemous name upon its heads. . . . And to it the dragon gave his power and his throne and great authority"* (Rev. 13:1,2).

Jesus Christ is the incarnate Word, the only begotten Son of Almighty God. *And He shares the power and throne and authority of His Father,* as Hebrews makes infinitely clear:

> *"He reflects the glory of God and bears the very stamp of his nature. . . . When he had made purification for sins, he sat down at the right hand of the Majesty on high. . ."* (Heb. 1:3,4).

*But just as Jesus is the embodiment of righteousness, so now, one is at the gate who is the essence of chaos and evil – **for the beast is to Satan what Jesus is to God!***

And before the world returns to the Holy One who created it, it will first quake under the fist of the Adversary: *". . . woe to you, O earth and sea, for the devil has come down to you in great wrath"* (Rev. 12:12).

For billions of years God nurtured the world which He spoke into existence. By His Word, it produced myriad millions of varieties of plants and animals, many so intricately fashioned as to be inconceivable to mere mortal imagination. But from Adam down to the present day, the Maker of Heaven and Earth has watched as those into whom He breathed the breath of life – *His breath -* have raped and pillaged and polluted the world which He placed in their care.

Earth is anathema. And now He wants His world back.

The great and terrible Day of the Lord is at hand.

The Battles Begin

In every era, the false shepherds and phony prophets – and now the rhinestone televangelists of our own day – have shamelessly pandered the word of God for a handful of silver. With the passage of the last tumultuous century and the beginning of this current and final one, the Book of Revelation particularly has become the object of their fallacious interpretations and prophecies. And because they do not have the answers, they attempt to make themselves appear mystical, clouding the truth at the expense of the sheep.

Revelation is indeed mystical. It was written so as to be understood only through the Spirit. God intentionally made it so to thwart those who quote and misuse the Scriptures for personal financial gain.

Even John did not – indeed he could not – comprehend the literal destruction that is going to befall our planet. God clothed it in rhetoric, and John repeated it flawlessly, but he did not understand. And even if he had, he would not have had the words in Hebrew or Aramaic or Greek to describe diseases and phenomena which have never happened since the beginning of the world.

Chapter one of Revelation serves as an introduction – the who, what, when, where and why of the book.

Chapters two and three are messages – which take the form of letters – from Jesus Christ to the angels of the seven churches of Asia. These seven letters detail the strengths and weaknesses – and the evils – which existed in the churches of John's day, and which have been mirrored in the churches of every era since. The conditional promises to believers at the conclusion of each letter are preceded by the phrase, *"To him who conquers. . . ."*

These seven messages were included here, at the beginning of Revelation, as a last-minute warning to the Christians of our day. A call to those who are awake and listening to repent of their sins and get ready for the red-hot fires of the tribulation which have already begun to burn and which are intensifying daily. Only those who conquer, by holding firm to their faith until the end, will receive a reward.

Chapter four sets forth the first of the specific events within the tribulation:

"After this I looked, and lo, in heaven an open door! And the first voice, which I had heard speaking to me like a trumpet, said, 'Come up hither, and I will show you what must take place after this" (Rev. 4:1).

And John was taken up into Heaven and stood before the throne. The One seated there held in His hand a scroll, sealed with seven seals, which only the Lion of the tribe of Judah, who is Christ, was found worthy to open. *And with the opening of the first seal, the wrath of God commenced:*

"And I saw, and behold, a white horse, and its rider had a bow; and a crown was given to him, and he went out conquering and to conquer" (Rev. 5:2).

Jesus is the first rider of what we have come to call the "Four Horsemen of the Apocalypse," and He leads His Father's end-time forces against evil. *This event has already taken place. It occurred at midnight on December 12, 1992. But most people missed it because they fell asleep. Spiritually speaking.*

Just look around you! Look at the signs of the times! You can see the tribulation has already begun and is worsening gradually, but at an ever-accelerating rate of speed.

In the prophetic book of *2 Esdras*, discussed at greater length in the next chapter, God sent His angel to Esdras (Ezra) to tell him of events which would take place during the tribulation:

106

1 *"Now concerning the signs: behold, the days are coming when those who dwell on earth shall be seized with great terror, and the way of truth shall be hidden, and the land shall be barren of faith.*

2 *And unrighteousness shall be increased beyond what you yourself see and beyond what you heard of formerly. . . .*

6 *And one shall reign whom those who dwell on earth do not expect, and the birds shall fly away. . . .*

8 *. . . fire shall often break out, and the wild beasts shall roam beyond their haunts, menstrual women shall bring forth monsters,*

9 . . . and all friends shall fight against one another; then shall reason hide itself, and wisdom shall withdraw into its storeroom.

10 *and it shall be sought by many but shall not be found, and unrighteousness and unrestraint shall increase on earth"* (2 Esdras 5:1,26,8-10).

One of the horrific examples of the increase in wickedness was carried nationwide by the media in the early months of 1999. The May 3, 1999 cover of *TIME* magazine, for one, bore the smiling image of two teenage boys. But underneath those two textbook boy-next-door faces the eerie caption – *reminiscent of the words of Esdras (verse 8) - blared: "The Monsters Next Door. . . ."*

Two boys, Eric Klebold and his friend Dylan Harris, gunned down one of their teachers, then killed twelve of their classmates and wounded 23 others in their neighborhood high school in

Littleton, Colorado. Both boys then committed suicide.

More than 400 incidents have occurred in the last decade, with some 400 wounded and over 200 killed (ABC7News.com>-school-shootings-how-many-shootings; Friday November 15, 2019).

The time will come in America when schools will resemble prison cells. Instead of doors, steel bars will lock students in and out of classrooms.

Why? Because today's youth live in a latchkey society that yawns at the profane, ridicules Christian values, places homosexuals in the pulpit, and passes out condoms instead of Bibles in the schools. Our nation turns a blind eye and a deaf ear to profanity and the gross immorality that proliferates across TV and movie screens, infiltrates the computers in our homes and invades an endless variety of personal electronic devices.

Speaking of the latter, the dangers simmering in today's digital technology teapot already dwarf the evils of all other media, exposing not only individuals, but the critical infrastructure of entire nations, to devastating cyber war attacks capable of crippling economies and launching wars – all at the hands of a few individuals sitting behind a desk almost anywhere in the world. Corporations, factories, banks, medical facilities, stock exchanges, transportation (including air traffic control systems), satellites and power grids, nuclear power plants, oil, gas and water companies, e-commerce businesses – and the military. All are at risk.

And no group is more aware of the dangers than the latter.

In June of 2009 the Secretary of Defense directed the Commander of the U.S. Strategic Command to establish the *U.S. Cyber Command*. USCYBERCOM – which became fully operational just a year later – is designed to direct operations in a realm of defense every bit as important as air, land – and space.

And speaking of space, in February of 2019 President Trump formally directed the Department of Defense to draft legislation creating a Space Force – a military branch that will conduct space warfare and other space operations. As of 2020, the United States is now the only country with an *independent space force.*

But returning to the events of the tribulation. . . . In December 1992, domestic terrorism arrived on our shores when Mir Aimal Kasi, a 28-year-old Muslim immigrant from Pakistan opened fire on employees at the main gate of the Central Intelligence Agency, killing two and wounding three others. Kasi told the court at his trial that the shooting was in retaliation for U.S. policies against Islamic nations. Kasi was also a suspect in the horrendous detonation which ripped through several floors of the World Trade Center in New York a month later (February 1993), killing six people and injuring more than 1,000. Six Muslim fundamentalists were eventually convicted for their part in that blast.

But the entire world recoiled in horror and shock on September 11, 2001, when 19 al-Qaeda-related terrorists hijacked four airplanes and crashed the first two into the Twin Towers of the World Trade Center and the third into The Pentagon. The abject cowardice of the hijackers was highlighted by the extraordinary heroism of the crew and passengers in the fourth plane, who crash-landed their flight in a Pennsylvania field while attempting to retake the plane and prevent it from reaching its target – forever immortalizing those brave souls who died on board in defense of their lives and homeland.

Al-Qaeda "accepted" the shame for these heinous acts. And ten years later (2011), the al-Qaeda leader responsible for the attacks died in Pakistan at the hands of an American military team.

But there is another, relatively new, form of terrorism to which we here in America are increasingly vulnerable – what the government refers to as Weapons of Mass Destruction or WMD. And all anyone has to do to find the information they need on nuclear, chemical, biological and radiological weapons is to go to the Internet.

Former Director of the CIA, James Woolsey, has said, *"Of all the threats that could inflict major damage to the U.S., terrorists using weapons of mass destruction is the threat for which the nation is least prepared"* (Livermore Study Group, June 1996). Meanwhile, world-wide trafficking in illegal nuclear materials is proliferating. And many countries hostile to ours – several of which are known to support terrorist groups – are developing WMD capabilities.

Dr. Vahid Majidi, who served as the Assistant Director for the WMD Directorate for the FBI from 2006 - 2012, stated unequivocally in 2011 that, *"The notion of probability of a WMD attack being low or high is a moot point because we know the probability is 100 percent. . . . There is going to be an attack using chemical, biological or radiological weapons. . . ."*

But with the escalation of barbaric acts of lawlessness here at home and abroad have come still other mighty signs of the times, including epidemic natural disasters and related events.

Two major motion pictures of the late 1990's, *Armageddon* and *Deep Impact,* reflected a frightening day in December 1997 when it appeared a mile-in-diameter asteroid might come terrifying close to (if not actually strike) Earth. Now NASA – and, yes, the new Space Force, are keeping a watchful eye on an asteroid named *Apophis,* set to pass unnervingly close to Earth on April 13, 2029. *That's Friday the 13th, in case you're interested.* And just to add to the excitement, *Apophis* was not only the Romanian deity who embodied *chaos,* but is even better known in ancient Egyptian religion as the **Great Serpent, enemy of the sun god** Ra.

Scientists have evidence it wouldn't be the first time one of these larger heavenly bodies has rammed into Earth. *Revelation says it's going to happen again.*

But even without the perils posed by these celestial events, our planet is ill at ease as other forces of Nature join the ever-increasing crescendo of record-breaking calamities felt around the world. Volcanoes, tornadoes, hurricanes, earthquakes, tsunamis. . . .

One such possibility that looms a little too close for comfort is Popocatepetl, *"Smoking Mountain."* A monster of a volcano at 17,883 feet, El Popo began to stir in 1993/1994. Evidence indicates it roars into action every thousand years or so, and its last significant eruption was over 800 years ago. A million cubic meter cauldron of magma roils just six miles below the mountain. *And some 20 million people, including those of Mexico City, the world's largest city, live within 50 miles of its base.* But the effects of such an eruption are not just localized. Ash and gases spewed from major eruptions reach the stratosphere, travelling the globe for weeks, or even years, affecting weather and climate. Sulfur-rich gases react with moisture in the atmosphere forming tiny droplets of sulfuric acid – which, along with ash particles, produce a haze that reduces sunlight and cools temperatures.

The 1980 eruption of Mount St. Helens is a constant reminder it can also happen again in our own backyard.

America also appears to be overdue for its next significant earthquake. In 2002 some 100 seismology experts (Working Group 02) issued a report stating there is a "62 percent probability of a **major, damaging earthquake** occurring in the greater San Francisco Bay Region over the next thirty years." *According to their estimate, we have barely ten years left.*

But 21st Century hurricanes have also left their mark on history, the worst being Katrina (August 2005). *Katrina racked up over $81 billion in property damages, making it the costliest natural disaster in the history of the United States.*

And around the world mind-rending natural disasters have claimed well over a million lives since the beginning of this millennium – the worst of which was the 2011 Fukushima Daiichi nuclear disaster which resulted from a 9.0 earthquake off Japan. Exact figures are unknown, but over 23,000 are believed to have been killed by the earthquake and resultant tsunami, and perhaps as many as another 10,000 are among the missing. As of 2016, five years of efforts to stop groundwater from continuing to get into the damaged reactor buildings and halt radioactive water from leaking into the Pacific Ocean have been unsuccessful. The event is expected to be the most costly natural disaster in world history, with the most recent estimates approaching as high as a trillion dollars!

But returning now to Revelation. . . . .

The first rider of the Four Horsemen has already gone out.

And from behind the *second seal* a bright red horse emerged. *"Its rider was permitted to take peace from the earth, so that people should slay one another, and he was given a great sword"* (Rev. 6:3-4).

The great sword is a violent assault of terrible events that have only just begun to come to pass. **It is the Sword of Islam!**

The first monstrous stroke of the Sword – as already mentioned – descended in all its insane, unbridled fury on the Twin Towers of the New York World Trade Center and The Pentagon – and on the bloody fields of Pennsylvania – in the morning hours of September 11, 2001. And the world reverberated under the impact.

Yet we had been warned! Before St. John was even born God had revealed to the Old Testament prophet-scribe Esdras (Ezra), in startling visions of the apocalypse, the hand that would wield the great sword:

> 28 *Behold, a terrifying sight, appearing from the east!*
>
> 29 *The nations of the dragons of Arabia shall come out with many chariots, and . . . their hissing shall spread over the earth, so that all who hear them shall fear and tremble.*
>
> 30 *Also the Carmonians, raging in wrath, shall go forth like wild boars of the forest, and with great power they shall come and engage them in battle and shall devastate a portion of the land of the*

Assyrians. . . .

35 *They shall throw themselves against one an-*
other and shall pour out a heavy tempest upon
the earth, and their own tempest; and there shall be
blood from the sword as high as a horse's belly. . .
(2 Esdras 15:28-30,35).

The sword brandished by the nations of the "dragons of Arabia" – *the Sword of Islam* – is the same great sword spoken of by John in Revelation 6:3,4. It is a sword consecrated at the hands of men whose irrational actions are born of an implacable hatred incapable of being analyzed or understood. And its profane appetite for blood will not be satiated for whatever measure of time remains.

As for verse 30 (above) which spoke of the Carmonians raging
*in wrath, **it is no coincidence that the boundaries of ancient Car-***
***mania coincide almost exactly with those of modern Iran** – an*
increasing threat to other nations of the Middle East.

The third seal was broken, and a black horse strode forth. Its rider had a balance in his hand, and a voice was heard crying, *"A quart of wheat for a denarius, and three quarts of barley for a denarius, and **do not harm the oil and wine**"* (Rev. 6:6).

As the fourth seal was opened, a pale horse appeared. Its rider's name was *Death,* and Hades followed. These two were given power over a fourth of the earth *to kill with sword, famine, pestilence, and by wild beasts.* These worldwide disasters include wars (both major and minor), famine/blight, germ warfare and diseases, AIDS and other viruses, widespread bacterial infections and similar organisms, and extraordinary plagues of insects.

The fifth seal revealed the tribulation martyrs – those who had thus far been killed for the witness they had borne for the Word of God. *They were told to rest until the number of their fellow servants was complete – those who were still alive on earth, but who were to be killed as they had been* (Rev. 6:9-11). This is further evidence that the "rapture" is the misleading product of wishful thinking. Comfortable Christianity is and always has been an oxymoron.

As the sixth seal was opened, the catastrophes hidden there were disclosed: a great earthquake, the sun became black, the full moon became like blood, and the stars fell to earth. The sky vanished like a scroll being rolled up, and all the mountains and islands were removed from their place. So great were these calamities that all of earth's inhabitants hid themselves in caves and up in the mountains, begging the rocks to fall on them and hide them from the wrath of God (Rev. 6:12-17).

These few verses herald cataclysmic events of unimaginable terrors which, since they all appear under the same seal, will occur very close in time to each other. Although only one great earthquake is mentioned here, earthquakes of great magnitude will be a constant occurrence during the tribulation – some so great that even mountains and islands will be moved out of their places.

The Sumatra earthquake in 2004 may have moved the seabed by as much as 100 feet. *But the greatest earthquake movement ever record by scientists occurred during the March 11, 2011 earthquake off Japan, previously referred to, when the sea floor shifted by 79 feet.*

Earthquakes which will take place in the last days are mentioned in four other verses in Revelation, as well as in Matthew 24:7, Mark 13:8 and Luke 21:11. But these and other calamities are perhaps most graphically described in the 24th chapter of Isaiah, where the prophet speaks of a time when the earth is split apart, its foundations tremble, the ground reels like a drunkard, its surface is twisted, *and it falls, never to rise again.*

But continuing with the events under the sixth seal (above): as for the sun becoming black and the full moon like blood, these phenomena will occur as massive worldwide thermonuclear explosions rock Earth.

Trillions of tons of dust and debris will be impelled into the atmosphere, where it will be picked up by the jet streams and swept around the world. Cloaked within these clouds, deadly viruses and other virulent organisms will encircle the globe and cause sickness, sores and open wounds.

There will be terrifying and deadly hemorrhagic viruses similar to Ebola Zaire, one of the most lethal currently known to man, whose victims suffer massive bleeding from every bodily orifice. Plagues will not only kill great masses of people, but also blot out plants, trees and crops from the face of the Earth.

Here and at other times during the tribulation, the stars will be dramatically affected – which will be more fully explained later.

Chapter seven is a brief interlude between the sixth and seventh seals. As John's apocalyptic visions continued, four angels stood at the four corners of the earth and held back the four winds from blowing on earth or sea or any tree. A fifth angel called to them and told them not to harm the earth or sea or trees *"until we have sealed the servants of our God..."* (Rev. 7:3; 9:4).

The "sealing" of the servants of God is simply an acknowledgement by God of those who are His own. And for a little time, the terror and destruction will cease, and the winds will be held back. That is, God will stop the jet streams – which stops the wind – which stops the proliferation of thermonuclear waste and viral and bacterial contamination – *temporarily. And mankind will have a very brief opportunity for repentance.*

As to the *great multitude which no man could number, from every nation,* which John saw standing before the throne in white robes, they are simply a mixed group of Christians. A few are martyrs; others are saved while the winds are held back.

Chapter eight begins with the opening of the seventh (and last) seal. Seven angels were given seven trumpets, each of which represents a series of impending disasters. Hail and fire mixed with blood fell on the earth, and a third of the earth and trees were burnt up, and all of the green grass (Rev. 8:7). These devastations will be partly as a result of the effects of the events under the preceding seal and partly as a result of new afflictions – *some of which will begin to occur before 2030.*

After this, a second angel blew his trumpet, and *"something like a great mountain"* – burning with fire – was thrown into the sea. A third of the sea turned to blood; a third of the sea creatures died; and a third of the ships were destroyed (Rev. 8:8,9).

These two verses foresee a great nuclear disaster, which will not be an accident, but which will set a huge piece of land on fire that will fall into the sea. This will be a catastrophe so horrendous it will destroy a third of the sea and its inhabitants – and a third of the ships in the area where it occurs.

Scripture does not reveal the area. But consider one possible location: the imposing sentinel which stands guard at the busy shipping gateway between the Atlantic Ocean and the Mediterranean Sea, where Africa (Morocco) and Europe (Spain) are only a stone's throw apart: *"The Rock" of Gibraltar, where 80,000 vessels pass through each year, including numerous nuclear submarines.*

Prized by the military for its strategic location, it was *"ne plus ultra"* to the ancient Romans – literally, *"no more beyond." The end of the world, beyond which the wise dared not venture.* A nuclear event here might just prove how visionary the Romans were.

The next trumpet is about to sound:

> 10 *The third angel blew his trumpet, and a great star fell from heaven, blazing like a torch, and it fell on a third of the rivers and on the springs of water.*
> 11 *The name of the star is Wormwood. A third of the waters became wormwood, and many people died from the water, because it had been made bitter* (Rev. 8:10,11).

The "great star" seen by John was originally plural, representing *two asteroids*. Though they are different from one another, they are yet one – like the Trinity is one. Hence, the singular form "star" was adopted. These asteroids are organic. Poisonous. They are not the same as Revelation 16:3,4. But they will hit land and water and affect both in much the way described a little earlier in this chapter. Tidal and shock waves will inundate coastlines, atmospheric conditions will be altered, and darkness will cover Earth for a time. There will be firestorms and earthquakes and further destruction to our already depleted ozone layer. *Even evolutionary changes will occur in their wake.*

As the fourth angel blew his trumpet . . . a third of the sun was struck, and a third of the moon, and a third of the stars, so that a third of their light might be darkened, and a third of the day might be kept from shining, and likewise a third of the night (Rev. 8:12).

This is a different happening from the third trumpet; the events of this verse will not be caused by the great asteroids of verses 10 and 11.

As Chapter nine commenced, the fifth angel blew his trumpet. John saw a star fallen from heaven to earth, and he (the "star") was given the key to the bottomless pit (Rev. 9:1,2). As he opened the shaft to the pit, locusts ascended to terrorize mankind. These locusts have as king over them an angel of Satan whose name in Hebrew is *Abaddon*. In Greek he is called *Apollyon,* and his name means *Destroyer* (Rev. 9:10,11). *Satan has at last come to realize that Earth, which he has held bound in sin since Adam and Eve turned it over to him, is about to slip from his grasp. And it is he who orders these supernatural creatures released.*

Unlike ordinary locusts, however, these are told not to harm the green growth of the earth. But, like scorpions, they are given power to torture – though not to kill - those who do not have the seal of God. *For five literal and terrifying months men will long to die, but death will elude them* (Rev. 9:1-6).

When a man or a woman is born of the spirit of God, he is "sealed" by God as one of His own. It is not a mark that is visible to the world, but rather a spiritual seal "visible" only to God and to other true Christians. And these scorpion-like locusts will have no power over those men and women who have truly been reborn of the spirit of God.

The sixth trumpet sounded, and four angels were released. These had been held ready for the exact moment in time to kill a third of mankind. With the angels, John saw a great calvary – riders on creatures resembling horses. And from them, fire and smoke and sulfur issued, which John called "three plagues," by which a third of mankind was to be killed. *These are cities burning, set on fire by God. By a process unknown to us, they will just start burning.*

But such is human nature that even now those who were not killed still did not repent of their murders or sorceries or immorality or thefts (Rev. 9:13-21).

How we have marveled through the years at those "good folks" who have told us they could never believe in a God who would let so many terrible things happen on Earth – *never for a moment considering we are the ones who, from the garden of Eden until now, have been responsible for the sickness and sorrow and evil that have come on mankind. God did not walk away from us; it is we who walked away from Him!*

Created over countless millennia by the patient hand of God, perfect in all its respects, our home – Earth - was the result of ultimate Wisdom and Power. A gift from the storehouse of His infinite love. Yet we have plundered and polluted it, physically and spiritually, from the very beginning, in flagrant violation of His commandments, which are good and holy.

As Chapter ten began, a mighty angel descended from Heaven. Standing with one foot on the sea and the other on land, he avowed there should be no more delay; but that, with the days of the seventh trumpet, which was about to sound, *"the mystery of God"* should be fulfilled, as foretold to His prophets (Rev. 10:1-11).

As the vision continued, John saw the temple of God and was told that it would be given over to the nations, and they would trample over the holy city for forty-two months.

During this period of time, God will grant His two witnesses power to prophesy for one thousand two hundred and sixty days (Rev. 11:2,3). And if anyone tries to harm them, fire pours from their mouth and consumes their foes (Rev. 11:5).

These are two extraordinary men who will travel the world - in person and on the media – preaching and prophesying. Those who seek their life are indeed doomed to be killed, for the fire that pours from their mouth is not a metaphor – it is literal. During the days of their prophesying, they will have power to hold back rain, to turn the waters into blood, and to smite the earth with every plague as often as they desire. Though they will perform only a few miracles, the few will be great.

These two witnesses will appear publicly before the beast. But when their testimony is finished, the beast – who comes from hell, but who will first be seen rising from the sea – *"will make war on them and conquer them and kill them, and their dead bodies will lie in the street of the great city . . . where their Lord was cruci-*

fied" (Rev. 11:7-10).

But at the end of three and a half days, a voice from Heaven called, *"Come up hither!"* And as they were carried up to Heaven in a cloud, an earthquake struck the city and seven thousand people were killed (Rev. 11:11-13).

Now the seventh trumpet sounded amidst signs and wonders in Heaven.

And as Chapter twelve opened, a great portent appeared in Heaven – a woman arrayed with the sun and moon and a crown of seven stars who was about to deliver a male child. A red dragon appeared before the woman, waiting to devour the baby. But the child, who is Jesus, was caught up to God, and the woman fled *"into the wilderness"* where *"she has a place prepared by God"* for a time.

The woman represents the true body of believers, who will be given strength and power to run and hide "in the wilderness" – literal and spiritual habitations – to get away from Satan during this time.

War followed in Heaven – the angels of God fighting against the dragon (Rev. 12:7). The dragon was thrown down to Earth and again pursued the woman – those true believers who are still here on earth during this time.

> 15 *The serpent poured water like a river out of his mouth after the woman, to sweep her away with the flood.*
> 16 *But the earth . . . opened its mouth and swallowed the river which the dragon had poured from*

his mouth.

17 Then the dragon became furious with the woman and went off to make war on the rest of her offspring, on those who keep the commandments of God and hold to the testimony of Jesus. . . (Rev. 12:15-17).

This is a great flood over a large location by which the devil seeks to destroy the believers. But there will be an instant splitting in the earth, which will literally swallow the flood.

Again, do not be misled: here in Chapter twelve, two-thirds of the way through the tribulation, Christians are still on the scene, as verse 17 just made infinitely clear.

Isaac Watts, whose enduring legacy of treasured hymns is unsurpassed in Christendom, put it this way in his immortal, *Am I A Soldier of the Cross?*—

> Am I a soldier of the cross,
> a Fol-l'wer of the Lamb,
> And shall I fear to own His cause,
> Or blush to speak His name?
>
> Must I be carried to the skies,
> On flowery beds of ease,
> While others fought to win the prize,
> and sailed thro' bloody seas?
> Are there no foes for me to face?
> Must I not stem the flood?
> Is this vile world a friend to grace,

To help me on to God?

Sure I must fight if I would reign;

Increase my courage, Lord;

I'll bear the toil, endure the pain,

Supported by Thy word.

Watts would have been appalled had he known that scarcely a hundred years after he penned this powerful hymn (c. 1724), little Scottish lassie Margaret MacDonald would propose the *"rapture"* – her easy-way-to-heaven escape route from the tribulation.

But continuing with John's visions of the end. . . .

Although the two witnesses were conquered – briefly – by the first beast, there are two "beasts" of Revelation.

And as *Chapter thirteen* unfolds, John steps slightly back in time to relate the first public appearance of each of these two sons of Satan and the events encompassing their disclosure to the world:

1 *And I saw a beast rising out of the sea, with ten horns and seven heads.* . . .

3 One of its heads seemed to have a mortal wound, but its mortal wound was healed, and the whole earth followed the beast with wonder.

4 *Men worshipped the dragon, for he had given his authority to the beast, and they worshipped the beast.* . . .

5 . . . and it was allowed to exercise authority for forty-two months;

6 it opened its mouth to utter blasphemies against

God. . . .

7 *Also it was allowed to make war on the saints and to conquer them.* And authority was given it over every tribe and people and tongue and nation,

8 and all who dwell on earth will worship it, every one whose name has not been written before the foundation of the world in the book of life of the Lamb that was slain. . . .

10 . . . *Here is a call for the endurance and faith of the saints.*

11 *Then I saw another beast which rose out of the earth; it had two horns like a lamb and it spoke like a dragon.*

12 *It exercises all the authority of the first beast in its presence, and makes the earth and its inhabitants worship the first beast.* . . .

13 It works great signs, even making fire come down from heaven to earth. . .

14 *and by the signs . . . it deceives those who dwell on earth, bidding them make an image for the beast which was wounded by the sword and yet lived;*

15 *and it was allowed to give breath to the image of the beast so that the image of the beast should even speak, and to cause those who would not worship the image of the beast to be slain.*

16 *Also it causes all, both small and great . . . to be marked on the right hand or the forehead,*

17 *so that no one can buy or sell unless he had the*

mark, that is, the name of the beast or the number
of its name.
18 This calls for wisdom; let him who has understanding reckon the number of the beast, for it is a
human number, its number is six hundred and sixty-six (Rev. 13:1,3-08,10-18.

Four times the Scriptures just quoted tell us the whole world
worshipped the dragon and the beast; and if they did not worship the image of the beast they were to be slain. But even before
John wrote Revelation, the Apostle Paul also spoke prophetically
of this world-wide worship of the beast – *"the son of perdition:"*

1 Now concerning the coming of our Lord Jesus
Christ *and our assembling to meet Him. . . .*
2 **Let no one deceive you in any way; for that day**
will not come, unless the rebellion comes first, and
the man of lawlessness is revealed, the son of per-
dition,
4 who opposes and exalts himself against every so-
called god or object of worship, so that he takes his
seat in the temple of God, proclaiming himself to be
God . . . (2 Thess. 2:1,3,4).

The two beasts are not related by blood. Initially, they are not going to know each other; nor are they going to be known to the general
public until the events set forth in the preceding verses of Revelation.
And neither of them had been born as of the first of 1999.

The beast whom John saw rising out of the sea will first be seen by the general populace as he comes off a military submarine. He is not a Jew, as some have proposed, but his father is a well-known religious leader.

In the 28th chapter of Ezekiel, this same son of Satan, who rises out of the sea, is referred to as the "prince of Tyre."

Tyre was once an important major port on the Mediterranean – a wealthy rocky island fortress just off the mainland of what is now Lebanon. Filled with pride and a false sense of security, she thought herself impregnable. Eventually submitting first to Assyrian authority and later to Babylonia, she ultimately was overrun by Alexander the Great after one of the most extraordinary sieges in history.

Thus, in *Ezekiel*, God compares the equally vain ***"prince of Tyre"*** – *the devil's spawn* – *to the city, and sets forth his eventual end in the same place where he is first seen, coming out of the sea.*

The word of the Lord came to me:

2 *"Son of man, say to the prince of Tyre, Thus says the Lord God: 'Because your heart is proud, and you have said, 'I am a god, I sit in the seat of the gods, in the heart of the seas,' yet you are but a man and no god. . . .'*

6 *therefore thus says the Lord God: 'Because you consider yourself as wise as a god,*

7 . . . *I will bring foreigners upon you, the most ruthless of the nations, and they shall draw their*

swords against the beauty of your wisdom and de-
file your splendor.

8 They shall thrust you down into the pit, and you
shall die the death of the slain in the heart of the
seas.

9 Will you still say, 'I am a god,' in the presence of
those who kill you. . . ?"

(Eze. 28:1,2,6-9).

But this same chapter of Ezekiel also contains the well-
known references to *Satan personally* **– whom God refers to as**
"the king of Tyre" **–**

11 Moreover the word of the Lord came to me:

12 "Son of man, raise a lamentation over the *king*
of Tyre, and say to him. . . .

13 You were in Eden, *the garden of God;* every pre-
cious stone was your covering. . . .

14 *With an anointed guardian cherub I placed you;*
you were on the holy mountain. . . .

15 You were blameless in your ways from the day
you were created, till iniquity was found in you.

16 . . . so I cast you as a profane thing from the
mountain of God, and the guardian cherub drove
you out.

17 *I cast you to the ground. . ."* (Eze. 18:11-17).

Satan's desire to make himself *"like the most high"* (Isa.

14:14) brought about his fall from the Paradise of God. But then he turned right around and used the same ploy here on earth, *"You will be like God"* (Gen. 3:5), he said, urging Eve to eat of the fruit of the forbidden tree.

God's singular response to each of these events was also remarkably similar. *For just as He used His anointed guardian cherub to drive the Adversary from His presence off His holy mountain (Eze. 18:16), so also He placed the guardian cherubim at the entrance to the earthly paradise of the garden of Eden when He drove out Adam and his wife after they sinned* (Gen. 3:24).

Who is this "guardian" of both Heaven and Earth – the "anointed" cherub who drove Satan from off the Holy Mountain, and who stands at the east of Eden, guardian of the way back into the presence of God on Earth? He is the *Christ* (Greek) and long-waited *Messiah* (Hebrew) – both of which mean *Anointed One* – who was consecrated from eternity to eternity as the median between Heaven and Earth, God and man:

"For there is one God, *and there is one mediator between God and men, the man Jesus Christ, who gave himself as a ransom for all. . ."* I Tim. 2:5).

But Satan, having been driven out of God's presence and triumphed over in the Cross by His Anointed Son, has waited through all the eons to this moment in time (Rev. 13) when he can place his progeny - the first beast of Revelation - in the temple of God on earth!

As to the beast's mortal wound which was healed (Rev. 13:3), it is a scar that looks as though it had been caused by a sword, but it was not. The beast caused it, and he also healed it – supernaturally. He has the power. It is a supernatural power which he has had from the beginning – that is, from birth.

For the beast is to Satan what Jesus is to God.

The second beast, which rose out of the earth, will first be observed publicly as he comes out of an underground military fortress. Photographers will be present at each of these two events (the first appearance of each man), and both men will become notorious.

But the two men look very, very different. One is very dark; the other is very light. The latter – the man who is light – is the one who comes out of the underground military fortress.

Verse 7 of *Chapter 13,* which referred to a time when the beast was allowed to make war on the saints and to conquer them, represents a special time in the tribulation – although this is not the only time the beast is to be allowed to war on the saints and to conquer them. But the forty-two months – the period of time in verse 5 – is an allegory. It is not literal.

The beast's authority will last only a few more than a dozen years. ***And although the beast will be able to do some miracles by the power of Satan, the "image' of the beast is computer generated. Smoke and mirrors. The image speaks and breathes, but it does not need air to survive.***

The Apostle Paul also foresaw these events and warned:

9 The coming of the lawless one by the activity of

Satan will be with all power and with pretended
signs and wonders,

10 and with all wicked deception for those who are
to perish, because they refused to love the truth and
so be saved.

11 Therefore God sends upon them a *strong delu-
sion* . . . (2 Thess. 2:9-11).

*The mark of the beast (Rev. 13:16-18) is a "number" which
is applied electronically, and it is in the body. But it is not "666";
this is another metaphor. The "number" represents the information the beast will have about people. There will be no alphabetical letters, rather – as in computer language – just numbers.*

As Chapter fourteen opened, John saw Christ (the Lamb)
standing on Mount Zion with 144,000 of those who had been redeemed from the earth and who follow the Lamb (Rev. 14:1,5).

These are the elect, the faithful of all generations. Several
angels followed, each with a special message. The second an-
nounced the fall of Babylon, and the third carried a warning that
anyone who worshipped the beast and received his mark would be
tormented with fire and sulfur forever (Rev. 14:14-20).

Afterward, *one like a son of man* (Jesus) and an angel were told
to take sickles and reap the harvest of the earth. As the vintage
was thrown into the great winepress of God, *blood flowed from
the press as high as a horse's bridle for about 200 miles* (Rev.
14:14-20).

The swinging of the sickles represents the ultimate time for
death and destruction to commence. The blood which flowed for

some 200 miles is metaphorical. It is the result of this last great outpouring of God's wrath.

Chapter fifteen heralded the appearance of seven angels with seven plagues. Each was given a golden bowl to pour out on the earth, and with them the wrath of God will be ended.

The bowls, like some of the other plagues and disasters of Revelation, were not written in complete chronological order. The effects of some parts of the tribulation will be felt well into the times of future disasters — much like a rolling snowball, which increases in size, speed and intensity as it races downhill, finally slamming into the area below and scattering its accumulated mass in all directions.

With the opening of *Chapter sixteen,* the first angel poured his bowl on earth, and "foul and evil sores" covered those who had received the mark of the beast (Rev. 16:2).

War, famine, fallout, and other devastations have left life weakened and vulnerable to each new wave of catastrophes. The sores are caused by worldwide diseases, many of which are unknown to us now, but which will become rampant because of the massive ravaging of the preceding years.

And as the second bowl was poured into the sea, it became like the blood of a dead man. Every living thing in the sea died (Rev. 16:3).

Then the third angel poured his bowl into the rivers and fountains, and they, too, became blood (Rev.16:4).

This is a part of the "snowball" effect – a concomitant result of the death and destruction caused by the preceding bowls – an extension of what has already been.

Though some might believe we are painting a picture of horrors too grim to be believed, man's merciless inhumanity to man has often exceeded belief. One such example is Uganda, where we ministered back in the late 1980's. It was not long after the blood-letting regime of Idi Amin Dada, a man accused of torture, cannibalism and the murder of hundreds of thousands of his own countrymen.

The exterior of our hotel in the capital city of Kampala was still riddled with bullet holes – acute reminders of the recent horrors that had ripped the "Pearl of Africa," as Winston Churchill once lauded it, into plasmic threads. And each night we were there our sleep was broken by the sporadic machine gun fire which still erupted – making us grateful our rooms were several stories above the ground.

"Blood literally ran in the streets of this city!" Our host in Uganda told us as we walked through downtown Kampala one morning. He pointed to the gutters along the side of the street. *"It filled up those drainage ditches and congealed before it could flow into the river."* Estimates of the number of people who were murdered or simply disappeared run as high as 500,000 (Amnesty International).

Yet Uganda was only an insignificant little incident by comparison with the utter devastation that is to come. Isaiah described it as a time when the stench would rise from the multitude of corpses and the mountains would flow with their blood (Isa. 34:3).

Part of the prophecy contained within the next bowl of Revelation had also first been uttered by Isaiah centuries earlier:

"The earth lies defiled under its inhabitants for they have transgressed the laws, violated the statutes. . . . Therefore a curse devours the earth, and its inhabitants suffer for their guilt. . . . the inhabitants of the earth are scorched and few men are left. . ." (Isa. 4:5,6).

And from the day Isaiah's oracle went out, God has been watching over His Word to perform it. For as the fourth angel of Revelation poured out his bowl on the sun –

> 8 . . . *it was allowed to scorch people with fire;*
> 9 *they were scorched by the fierce heat; and they cursed the name of God who had power over these plagues. They did not repent and give him the glory* (Rev. 16:8,9).

As the atmosphere becomes ever more transparent to solar and UV/UVR radiation, we face not only the scorching heat, but also increased susceptibility to skin diseases, cancers, eye damage, and – according to recent research – suppression of the body's immune system to chemical sensitivities and infectious disease.

Bacteria have clearly demonstrated their remarkable ability to mutate and grow increasingly resistant to antibiotics. According to the Infectious Disease Society of America's website, antibiotic-resistant infections not only add *$20 billion annually to the burden of the U.S. health care system, but also increase total patient hospital stays by more than 8 million days!*

A May 18, 2016 internet report (36321394) by James Gallagher, Health Editor of the BBC News website, quotes a global review as stating, *"Superbugs will kill someone every three seconds by 2050 unless the world acts now"* in the battle against antimicrobial resistance. Not only are we improperly using the drugs we already have, but we are failing to develop enough new antibiotics to combat resistant infections. *Not four years later, along came the present epidemic - coronavirus!*

As of 2020 estimates place the world's population at some 7.8 billion people. Just a little over forty years ago *it was half that*. And by 2050, at the current growth rate, the number would exceed 12 billion, the majority of which would come from poor countries which can't even cope with their current population.

With all this the end is not yet. John's visions continue as the fifth bowl was poured out on the throne of the beast.

The darkness of 16:10 is spiritual, but the pain and sores of the following verse are the result of diseases not yet "invented."

The sixth bowl, when it was emptied, caused the waters of the Euphrates to dry up. *This is literal.*

And as John looked, he saw evil spirits, sent out by the dragon and his beast, going abroad –

> 14 . . . *to the kings of the whole world, to assemble them for battle on the great day of God the Almighty. . . .*
> 16 *And they assembled them at the place which is called in Hebrew Armageddon* Rev. 16:14,16).

Armageddon is a metaphor which appears nowhere in the Bible except here in Revelation 16:16.

It is not a battle fought by armies in a valley somewhere. Rather, it is a symbolic term chosen by God for this final conflict – a worldwide "battle" in which everybody will fight everybody, a battle which has already commenced.

"For what?" You ask.

No one will know!

A "blindness" has simply come on the world.

Only an evanescent moment in time remained as the seventh angel emptied his bowl into the air, and a voice from the throne was heard calling out, "It is done!"

The last worldwide devastations were ushered in by an earthquake of such titanic proportions its like had never been since the beginning of mankind. *It rent the earth; the cities of the nations fell; "every island fled away, and no mountains were to be found; and great hailstones dropped on men from heaven. . ."* (Rev. 16:17-20), as God poured out the final virulent dregs from the cup of his wrath.

To fully explain the events of these last few verses we must return to the calamities concealed behind the sixth seal, which are similar to those quoted above: *". . . there was a great earthquake, and the sun became black as sackcloth, the full moon became like blood, and the stars of the sky fell to the earth as the fig tree sheds its winter fruit when shaken by a gale. The sky vanished like a scroll that is being rolled up, and every mountain and island was removed from its place"* (Rev. 6:12-14).

Some 2,700 years earlier, Isaiah (740 B.C. – 687 B.C.) foretold the portents of these few remaining days of the tribulation when the celestial bodies will not give their light, the heavens will tremble, and the earth will be shaken out of its place by the wrath of God (Isa. 13:9,10,13).

Much later, while the Lord Jesus was here on earth, He confirmed Isaiah's prophecies and the signs which would immediately precede His second advent, saying:

> 21 For then there will be great tribulation, such as has not been from the beginning of the world until now, no, and never will be. . . .
>
> 29 Immediately after the tribulation of those days the sun will be darkened, and the moon will not give its light, and the stars will fall from heaven, and then all the tribes of the earth will mourn, and they will see the Son of man coming on the clouds of heaven . . .
>
> 31 and he will send out his angels with a loud trumpet call, and they will gather his elect from the four winds, from one end of heaven to the other (Matt. 24:21,29-31).

At the end (verse 29), God is going to change the power that holds the heavenly bodies in space. There will be a sudden, galaxy-wide alteration of the gravitational fields, and great numbers of galaxies and even universes are going to leave their places. This is why the stars appear to "fall," as John also prophesied in Revelation 6:12-14.

Paul declared of Christ, *"He is before all things, and in him all things hold together"* (Col. 1:17). Similarly, Hebrews 1:3 says Jesus not only reflects the glory of God, but is the exact imprint of His Father's nature and "upholds the universe by the word of his power."

And that same "Word of Power" that spoke the universe with all of its galaxies into existence in the beginning and hung them in place throughout infinite space will once more speak to His Creation. And on His Word, they will literally be shaken out of their positions.

To put it another way, He is going to withdraw His Power – the restraining power that holds the celestial bodies in place – and allow them to move in all directions. Universal chaos will result. It will be like bumper cars at a carnival, and the consummation will be utter desolation. And when the celestial bumper cars are all gone, the sky will appear to vanish like a scroll rolled up (Rev. 6:14) – simply because there will not be anything left to see.

The next two chapters – seventeen and eighteen – are devoted exclusively to the judgment and fall of *"Babylon,"* which John alternately refers to as, *"the great harlot who is seated upon many waters," "the great city"* or *"the woman sitting on a scarlet beast."*

The use of the city name *"Babylon"* is figurative. *It is not to be associated with ancient Rome – an empire which today lays encrusted in the dusty chronicles of yesteryear, its glory departed, its prophetic relevance long concluded.*

Far from representative of any single earthly city, the spiritual profundity of Babylon – partially perceptible from the first verse of Chapter 17 – is indeed much vaster:

> *"Then one of the seven angels . . . said to me, 'Come, I will show you the judgment of the great prostitute*

who is seated upon many waters'. . ." (Rev. 17:1).

The *many waters* on which the harlot is seated, the angel explained, represent a far-flung assemblage of many peoples and nations and tongues (17:15) – indicating *the global extent* of the harlot Babylon's great power and influence.

The gravity of the city's sins and the reason for her impending doom are emphasized by the fact that they are twice stated – once in each of the two chapters:

> *"And I saw the woman, drunk with the blood of the saints, the blood of the martyrs of Jesus"* (Rev. 17:6).
> *"And in her was found the blood of prophets and of saints. . . "* (Rev. 18:24).

The Old Testament provides ample clues to the identity of Babylon (see Malachi 2:1-9), as does the New Testament Book of Matthew. The latter devotes the twenty-third chapter to Jesus' castigation of those who, by their actions, make Babylon their mother.

"Blind fools." He rebuked them. *"Hypocrites and blind guides!"*

They were the religious zealots of His and every other age who preached but did not practice, faithless teachers who sought the places of honor in the synagogues, but who – by their false piety – led the sheep away from the Kingdom of Heaven:

> 31 "Thus you witness against yourselves that you are sons of those who murdered the prophets. . . .

34 Therefore I send you prophets and wise men and scribes, some of whom you will kill and crucify, and some you will flog in your synagogues and persecute from town to town,

35 so that on you may come all the righteous blood shed on earth. . ." (Matt. 23:31,34,35).

Babylon, mother of harlots, is the false church. The architect of organized religion. Within her rebellious streets flows not only the blood of the prophets and saints, but also that of God's own son – the Author of Life, who came to say, *"I love you,"* to a world that refused to care!

God's own – *His people* – have continually reveled in apostasy and, like a faithless wife, played the harlot.

And just as literal Babylon, once the mightiest of Earth's cities, was overthrown and by the Word of God never rebuilt – *"Because of the wrath of the Lord it shall not be inhabited, but it shall be wholly desolate"* (Jer. 50:13 KJV) – so also shall spiritual Babylon, the corrupt universal church of Revelation, *"be thrown down with violence, and shall be found no more. . ."* (Rev. 18:21).

She will perish from the same violence by which the world is consumed. But a double portion of God's wrath has been decreed on "Babylon" because she – of all the peoples on earth – should have remembered her Husband and Maker.

Thus, the cry goes out to those who are able to hear:

"Come out of her, my people, lest you take part in her sins, lest you share in her plagues" (Rev. 18:4).

No words can express the unutterable significance of the forgoing verse. *It is God's last personal warning to man in the Bible — and it is directed exclusively to His people within the house that is called by His name:*

"Come out of her my people. . . . "

Come out of the harlot, the false church, and worship God in spirit and in truth. Set yourselves apart from those who have a form of religion, but who are without faith or power. Leave the churches that substitute their doctrines of convenience for the doctrines of God, and who produce no fruit for the Kingdom of Heaven. Come out of the world religious councils whose machinations puff their own agendas and not those of the living God. Separate yourselves from men who put good for evil and evil for good.

"Come out of her, my people, lest you take part in her sins, lest you share in her plagues."

Remember also the words of warning spoken by the Apostle Peter, whom Jesus personally chose to lead His first church in Jerusalem after His ascension:

". . . judgment begins with the house of God" (I Peter 4:17).

When Jesus walked among men, His only display of physical force came when He entered the House of God and found it overflowing with *merchants* selling oxen and sheep and pigeons. He drove them out of the synagogue, overturned the tables of the money changers, and admonished them all: *"Take these things away; do not make my Father's house a house of trade"* (John 1:4-16).

Chapter 18 of Revelation provides a striking analogy. It describes in depth the "merchants" of the earth who have grown rich on the wantonness and material appetites of the harlot Babylon. Now the judgment of God has fallen on her. And as she burns, the merchants stand far off, weeping and mourning. The mother of harlots has been laid waste and no longer buys their costly goods: frankincense and myrrh, gold, jewels and fine linen, wine and oil, scented wood and human souls. . . (Rev. 18:11-19.)

God has avenged on Babylon the blood of His servants.

Chapter 19 resounds with the voice of a multitude in Heaven praising God and calling the righteous to the *"marriage supper of the Lamb and his Bride"* (Rev. 19:7-9) – those men and women for whom the holy city New Jerusalem has been prepared.

Afterward, a white horse appeared with "The Word of God" astride, and John reiterated Jesus' status as leader of His Father's end-time forces – those who have kept the faith in this final War of right against wrong (Rev. 19:11-16).

Then an angel appeared, standing in the sun, and called the birds of the air to a different feast – *"the great supper of God"* (Rev. 19:17,18) – a feast on the flesh of all those who fought against the rider of the white horse and His army. *In vivid language John evokes a symbolic picture of worldwide carnage and the utter destruction of the wicked. As the righteous were invited to the marriage supper of the Lamb and to everlasting life, so now those who have done evil were condemned to "the great supper of God" which is eternal punishment.*

The first beast and the false prophet (the second beast) are captured and thrown into the lake of fire – a figure of speech for the second death (19:20; 20:14; 21:8) - to be tormented day and night forever (20:10).

As Chapter 20 opened, an angel descended from Heaven with the key to the bottomless pit and a great chain with which Satan was bound. The pit was shut and sealed over the perfidious engineer of man's Fall to keep him from deceiving the nations *"for a thousand years."* But after that he must be loosed again *"for a little while"* (Rev. 20:1-3).

The thousand years do not represent a literal period of time; rather, it will be a season of approximately one year when there is no activity by Satan.

The vision continued; thrones appeared on which were seated those to whom judgment was committed. And John saw the souls of those who had been beheaded for their testimony to Jesus and who had not worshipped the beast or received its mark. These saints came to life and reigned with Christ *"a thousand years."* This is the "first resurrection" (20:4-6).

But as in verses 20:1-3, these few verses do not herald a literal one thousand year reign of Jesus and believers here on Earth. The Apostle Paul made this infinitely clear – even declaring he spoke *"by the word of the Lord"* – when he described the resurrection of the dead at the return of Christ, and their catching up into the clouds, along with the saints who are alive and left on Earth until His coming:

15 *For this we declare to you by the word of the Lord, that we who are alive, who are left until the coming of the Lord, shall not precede those who have fallen asleep.*

16 *For the Lord himself will descend from Heaven. ... And the dead in Christ will rise first;*

17 *then we who are alive, who are left, shall be caught up together with them in the clouds to meet the Lord in the air; and so we shall always be with the Lord* (I Thess. 4:15-17).

How much time elapses between these two ascensions, if any, is unclear, but two things are readily apparent. First, Paul's language obviously indicates it was not a protracted period of time. And second, Jesus plainly does not set foot on earth. *Both the dead — who are said to rise first — and then those who are alive on earth at His coming — are caught up* **together,** *"to meet the Lord* **in the air."**

As to the "thousand years," remember, Peter — in speaking strictly of the last days and the approach of the Second Advent of Christ — confirmed that the number of days and years set forth in the Scriptures are not always literal:

7 *But by the same word the heavens and earth that now exist have been stored up for fire, being kept until the day of judgment and destruction of ungodly men.*
8 *But do not ignore this one fact, beloved, that with the Lord one day is as a thousand years, and a thousand years as one day.* . . (2 Peter 3:7,8).

To reiterate: *there is not going to be a time when the faithful mentioned in Revelation 20:4 will reign on earth for a literal period of one thousand years — with or without Christ. The thousand years mentioned in 20:2-5 are symbolic of only one year in actual time – the year 2069 – the last year before the end comes. Those who come to life here are a special group. They are the martyrs of all generations – those Christians who have been murdered for their testimony of the Word of God. They will have the authority of Christ, and they will reign on Earth for one year, during which time there will be no activity by Satan.*

Before he was martyred for his unswerving faith, Isaiah foresaw this time and prophesied:

> 21 On that day the Lord will punish the host of heaven, in heaven. . . .
> 22 They will be gathered together as prisoners in a pit; they will be shut up in a prison, and *after many days* they will be punished (Isa. 24:21,22).

Note that Isaiah says, "after many days" – not after a thousand years.

Then, at the end of a one-year period of peace, Satan will be loosed,

> 8 . . . and will come out to deceive the nations which are at the four corners of the earth, that is, Gog and Magog, to gather them for battle; their number is like the sand of the sea (Rev. 20:8).

Here in Revelation, "Gog and Magog" are simply metaphors for the whole world; and, similarly, the "battle" is a metaphor for this final conflict of righteousness versus evil.

"And they marched up over the broad plain of the earth and surrounded the camp of the saints and the beloved city, but fire came down from heaven and consumed them . . ." (Rev. 20:9).

God called it a "camp" because it is a camp – a temporary habitation of saints here on earth.

And as for "the beloved city," it is, ". . . *the city of our God . . . the mountain of His holiness"* (Psa. 48:1).

During this brief time of violence, the saints will once more have to protect themselves. But God will come to the aid of His people, and fire will literally come down from Heaven. The enemy will be consumed, and Satan will forever be consigned to a hell of his own making.

As John's visions neared their end, a great white throne appeared; and before the presence of the One seated there, earth and sky fled away. The books were opened; the dead were judged; and those whose names were not found in the book of life were thrown into the lake of fire.

Chapters 21 and 22 are devoted primarily to the new Heaven and new Earth and to a description of the holy city, New Jerusalem. The first Heaven and Earth have passed away. And here, in the final two chapters of Revelation, John sees the New Jerusalem *coming down out of heaven from God* (21:2), its transcending beauty beyond human imagining.

For the time being we live in a physical world. But one day we will graduate to a spiritual realm – a new dimension we have yet to experience. The Apostle Paul said our present bodies will be changed (I Cor. 15:51-54). But so will all things – trees, flowers, the whole of creation. Everything is going to be new and vastly different. But not just in appearance. For the new Earth – that is, the New Jerusalem – is many things, both physical (the things that are seen) and spiritual. Spiritual because the city that is coming is also God's kingdom. And only the redeemed shall walk there (Rev. 21:17).

John was given a rod of gold to measure the city, which is strangely in the geometrical form of a cube (21:15,16): *its length, breadth and height are equal* – each being a distance of twelve thousand stadia (about fifteen hundred miles).

All earthly cities are a plane. That is, they lie "flat" with only two dimensions – length and breadth. But the holy city is cubic – something like a great mammoth building. *It is multi-dimensional, dimensions unfamiliar to earth existing within other dimensions.*

Revelation closes with the reaffirmation by Christ himself, in almost the identical words of Revelation 1:1: *". . . the Lord, the God of the spirits of the prophets, has sent his angel to show his servants what must soon take place. And behold, I am coming soon"* (Rev. 22:6,7).

CHAPTER TEN

THE END OF TIME

INTRODUCTION:

The New Testament begins with the four gospels – Matthew, Mark, Luke and John – each of which details the life of Christ from the viewpoint of the author. Two of these, Matthew and Luke, include the genealogy of Jesus.

Genealogy was of the utmost importance to the Hebrews. Old Testament prophecy clearly stated God's Anointed One would come through the lineage of Abraham and David. And it was therefore necessary at the onset of the New Testament to set out a definitive line of descent for the Lord's Christ through these two men.

Matthew 1:1 begins: *"The book of the genealogy of Jesus Christ, the son of David, the son of Abraham. Abraham was the father of Isaac, and Isaac the father of Jacob. . . . ,"* and on forward through the generations to, *"Joseph the husband of Mary, of whom Jesus was born. . ."* (Matt. 1:16).

Luke (3:23-38), on the other hand, reverses the order. He first sets out Jesus as *"being the son (as was supposed) of Joseph,"*

(3:23), and then proceeds to trace His lineage back in time to *". . . Adam, the son of God . . ."* (John 3:38; Genesis 5) – upon whom the Creator first bestowed a personal relationship through a knowledge of Himself.

It is in Genesis 5 that the biblical record of genealogy begins in detail, saying, *"This is the record of the descendants of Adam. . ."*, and continuing onward for fifteen hundred years, through the sons and grandsons of Adam, all the way to the birth of Noah and his three sons, Shem, Ham and Japheth.

Following the Flood and the death of Noah, Genesis 10 and 11 set forth an extensive *second* genealogical record – this time of Noah's sons – and note, *"from these the nations spread abroad on the earth after the flood* (Gen. 10:32)."

And so the generations of the biblical line of descent continue unbroken to Abraham and his son Isaac, and to Isaac's son Jacob (whom God renamed "Israel"). It was the twelve sons of the latter who would come to be referred to as the twelve tribes of Israel. Of these tribes, two are the best known: **Judah**, through whom King David and eventually Jesus would come, and **Levi,** the tribe which God set apart as His own and consecrated to serve as priests and to perform duties associated with the tabernacle. Duties so sacred that anyone who attempted to minister before God other than a Levite was sentenced to die.

Into this latter tribe was born **Ezra**, from whom the fifteenth book of the Old Testament takes its name. And since the books of **Ezra** and **Nehemiah** (the sixteenth book of the Old Testament) were originally one scroll, Ezra may have been the author of both. **Of equal significance is that Jewish tradition**

also holds Ezra to be the author of *I and II Chronicles*. But a number of the books of the **Apocrypha** also bear the name **"Esdras"** – the Latin variation for Ezra. The fact that the prophet's lineage is carefully set out in *Ezra 7 and in 2 Esdras 1*, and that he is repeatedly designated in these books as *prophet, priest and scribe*, are also indicators of the reverential respect accorded him. Descended from Aaron, the first high priest of Israel, Ezra is venerated by Jewish tradition as the *"Father of Judaism."*

And it was to Ezra that the primary keys to unlock the mystery of the year of Christ's return were given.

THE APOCALYPSE OF 2 ESDRAS:

In the fourteenth chapter of *2 Esdras*, the Lord calls to Esdras to tell him of the times of the end:

> 10 For the age has lost its youth, and the times begin to grow old.
> 11 *For the age is divided into twelve parts and nine of its parts have already passed,*
> 12 *as well as half of the tenth part; so **two of its parts remain, besides half of the tenth part***" (2 Esdras 14:10-12).

In speaking of the divisions of time, God obviously was not talking about the uncharted eons which rolled before the birth of Adam – those billions of years during which our

Earth originated and developed. For how could He have divided the "unknown" into twelve parts? Rather, He arbitrarily established a comprehensible time frame – that is, a specific number of years – for the whole of "time." *Those years began with the birth of Adam, His first elect, in 3930 B.C., and they include the period of time within which the events described in the Bible occurred — or will occur – from Adam to Revelation.*

Each of the twelve divisions of the whole of time represents a one-thousand year period of time, which will be explained more completely a little later in this chapter.

Thus, the "whole of time," according to God's unique plan, is 12,000 years.

But – but – God's blue print for the ages of time has a "twist:" **One-half of this time is literal; the other half is spiritual.**

Why did He do it this way? You'll have to ask Him.

In any event, the *Timelines of Adam* (following page) is a graph of the *literal half – that is, 6,000 years*.

Column one sets forth the name of a person or an event in biblical history. Column two is the number of years that individual was born or the event occurred *after Adam's birth*. Column three is the number of years the individual was born or the event occurred *before or after the birth of Christ*. And column four contains information relevant to a specific year or period of time.

Example: Seth (second name from top) was born 130 years *after* the birth of Adam – but 930 years *before* Christ's birth.

EVENT	YEARS AFTER ADAM	YEARS FROM CHRIST		NOTES
Birth of Adam	0	3930	B.C.	
Birth of Seth	130	3800	B.C.	Adam's age at birth of Seth
Birth of Enosh	235	3695	B.C.	Adam's age at birth of Enosh
Birth of Kenan	325	3605	B.C.	Adam's age at birth of Kenan
Birth of Mahalalel	395	3535	B.C.	Adam's age at birth of Mahalalel
Birth of Jared	460	3470	B.C.	Adam's age at birth of Jared
Birth of Enoch	622	3308	B.C.	Adam's age at birth of Enoch
Birth of Methuselah	687	3243	B.C.	Adam's age at birth of Methuselah
Birth of Lamech	874	3056	B.C.	Adam's age at birth of Lamech
Death of Adam	930	3000	B.C.	Adam's age at death
Birth of Noah	1056	2874	B.C.	Years after Adam/Before Christ
Birth of Noah's sons	1556	2374	B.C.	Shem Ham Japheth Gen. 5:32
FLOOD	1656	2274	B.C.	Gen. 5:27, 7:6
Birth of Arpachshad	1658	2272	B.C.	Son of Shem/Gen. 11:10
Birth of Shelah	1694	2236	B.C.	Son of Arpachshad
Birth of Eber	1724	2206	B.C.	Son of Shelah
Birth of Peleg	1758	2172	B.C.	Son of Eber
Birth of Reu	1788	2142	B.C.	Son of Peleg
Birth of Serug	1820	2110	B.C.	Son of Reu
Birth of Nahor	1850	2080	B.C.	Son of Serug
Birth of Terah	1879	2051	B.C.	Son of Nahor
Birth of Abram	1949	1981	B.C.	1st named of Terah's sons/Gen 11:26
Abram goes to Canaan	2024	1906	B.C.	Abram 75 years old/Gen. 12:4
Birth of Isaac	2049	1881	B.C.	Abram 100 years old/Gen. 21:5
Birth of Jacob/Esau	2109	1821	B.C.	Twins - Gen. 25:26
Death of Abraham	2124	1806	B.C.	175 years old/Gen. 25:7
Death of Isaac	2229	1701	B.C.	180 years old/Gen. 35:28
Jacob goes to Egypt	2239	1691	B.C.	130 years old/Gen. 47:9
Exodus under Moses	2484	1446	B.C.	ISBE Vol 1, p 44, Eerdman's
Solomon dies	3000	930	B.C.	I Kings 6:1
Destruction of Jerusalem	4000	70	A.D.	Temple destroyed
Christ's Return	6000	2070	A.D.	6000 years after Adam

Only the last event has not yet come to pass: the Second Coming of Christ. And while the exact hour and day of His return are still unknown (Mark 13:32), the year is not: Jesus will return in 2070 A.D., exactly 6,000 years after Adam's birth.

In speaking of the literal 6,000 year period, God sent a vision of the last days to Ezra (Esdras). He sees a woman in terrible distress. She tells him she was childless through thirty years of marriage, but then God granted her a son. He grew to manhood, but on the day of his wedding he died; and the woman is in great mourning because of his death. As Ezra attempts to comfort her, she utters a cry that shakes the earth. Ezra no longer sees the woman, but a city. And God sends an angel to the bewildered prophet to give him the interpretation of what he has seen.

> 44 "This woman whom you saw, whom you now see as an established city, is Zion.
> 45 And as for her telling you that she was barren for **thirty years**, it is because there were **3,000 years** in the world before any offering was offered in it.
> 46 . . . . after three thousand years Solomon built the city and offered offerings; then it was that the barren woman bore a son.
> 47 And as for her telling you that she brought him up with much care, that was the period of residence in Jerusalem.
> 48 And as for her saying to you, *'When my son entered his wedding chamber, he died,'* and that misfortune had overtaken her, that was the destruction that befell Jerusalem'" (2 Esdras 10:44-48).

Note that in verse 45 the angel tells Ezra there were 3,000 years in which sacrifices (offerings) were not yet offered in Zion

(Jerusalem). It had been the desire of Solomon's father David, the second king of Israel, to build a house of worship in Jerusalem. But God told David the building of the temple would be entrusted to his son Solomon (by Bathsheba). And so it happened that *"after the 3,000 years, Solomon build the city and offered the sacrifices."*

And as you will note on the Timelines, Solomon died in 930 B.C. – precisely 3,000 years after the birth of Adam!

Verse 47 refers to the period of time following construction of the temple and the death of Solomon: *"that was the period when Jerusalem was inhabited."* For a thousand years Jerusalem remained the center of religious worship for the Jews. It was during this time that Jesus Christ was born in Bethlehem and ultimately crucified on a hill outside Jerusalem.

But then (verse 48), *"destruction . . . overtook Jerusalem."*

This prophesy was fulfilled in 70 A.D. – exactly 1,000 years after Solomon's death – when the Romans sacked Jerusalem and destroyed the Temple of Solomon! And from 70 A.D. to 2070 A.D. (when Christ will return), there are exactly 2,000 more years.

A grand total of 6,000 literal years from the birth of Adam!

In the early years of our schooling, we are taught to "cross-check" the answers to math problems for accuracy. So now let's double-check the correctness of God's plan for the ages.

The visions recorded in *2 Esdras* came to the prophet in 450 B.C. while he and his countrymen, the Israelites, were captives in Media during the reign of King Artaxerxes (who, incidentally, held the prophet-scribe in high regard).

Ezra was in anguish over the evils that had befallen Israel at the hands of a nation he believed more wicked than his own. As he sought to reconcile God's justice and goodness with the suffering of his people, an angel was sent to help him understand the ways of God and to tell him of the times of the end.

Remember, Ezra had been told, *"the age has lost its youth, and the times begin to grow old. For the age is divided into twelve parts, and nine of its parts have already passed, as well as half of the tenth part; so two of its parts remain, besides half of the tenth part"* (2 Esdras 14:10-12).

To put it another way, out of the twelve divisions of time (*think spiritually*) only two and a half remained:

Two and a half is 21 percent of the twelve parts of time;
And 21 percent of 12,000 years equals 2,520 years.
Ezra wrote 2 Esdras in 450 B.C.
And between 450 B.C. and 2070 A.D. there are 2,520 years!

It could not be more clear that time is running out:

2,520 years (21 percent of the "whole of time")
-2,470 years (years elapsed from 450 B.C. to 2020 A.D.)
=   50 years remaining until 2070 A.D. and the end of time

But that's still not all! For the **Epistle of Barnabas** – *one of the early Church letters – contains two additional keys to the mystery of time. The "keys" are presented in the form of allegories – that is, a symbol in a story or a poem that can be used to convey a meaning which is different from that which the words first appear to impart.*

Barnabas accompanied the Apostle Paul on the first of his missionary journeys. Like Esdras before him, Barnabas was of the priestly tribe of Levi. And since the Levites had been specifically entrusted by God with all matters relating to the spiritual life of the Hebrews, it is therefore not surprising to find Barnabas instructing the readers of his epistle on the *spiritual implications of the Sabbath.*

1 Furthermore it is written concerning the sabbath in the Ten Commandments, which God spake in the Mount Sinai to Moses, face to face; Sanctify the sabbath of the Lord with pure hands, and with a clean heart.

2 And elsewhere he saith; If thy children keep my sabbaths, then will I put my mercy upon them.

3 And even in the beginning of the creation he makes mention of the sabbath. And God made in six days the work of his hands; *And he finished them on the seventh day, and he rested the seventh day, and sanctified it.*

4 **Consider, my children, what that signifies, he finished them in six days. The meaning of it is this, that in six thousand years the Lord God will bring all things to an end. For with him one day is as a thousand years; as himself testifieth, saying, Behold this day shall be as a thousand years. Therefore, children, in six days, that is, in six thousand years, shall all things be accomplished** (Epistle of Barnabas 15:1-4).

Alternate translations from Greek, including one by J. B. Lightfoot (1828-1889) – English theologian, noted author of several commentaries, and Bishop of Durham – render verse 5, *". . . in six days, that is, in six thousand years, everything shall come to an end."*

Here in these four verses Barnabas unequivocally stated – not once, but twice – *that where the Scriptures declare that God completed the creation in six days, it signifies that in six thousand years all things shall be accomplished, and the Lord God will bring all things to an end!*

Moses, as we know, died some 1,500 years before the New Testament days of Barnabas came to pass. **Exodus 33:11 says:** *"Moses was a man with whom God spoke 'face to face, as a man speaks to his friend.'"* **And Moses observed,** *"For a thousand years in thy sight are but as yesterday when it is past. . ."* (Psa. 90:40).

Some nine centuries later, give or take a few decades, God revealed to Ezra, *". . . I told him (Moses) many wondrous things, and showed him the secrets of the times and declared to him the end of the times. Then I commanded him, saying, 'These words you shall publish openly, and these you shall keep secret'"* (2 Esdras 14:5,6).

It was on Peter that the mantle of leadership fell in the first church in Jerusalem immediately following the resurrection and ascension of Jesus. And Peter, in a discourse regarding the *Second Coming,* repeated the familiar refrain:

> "But do not ignore this one fact, Beloved, that with the Lord one day is as a thousand years, and a thousand years as one day" (II Peter 3:8).

So it was that throughout the great passages of time, God *repeatedly* declared in the Scriptures through His chosen prophets that with Him one day is as a thousand years, so that at the appointed time this mystery might be revealed to us: ***that the six days of Creation signify that 6,000 years after Adam God "will bring all things to an end."***

Yet the thirteenth chapter of the *Epistle of Barnabas* (verses 3 and 4 are restated below) has still more to tell us. *Applied as an allegory, verse 3 reveals a second truth within the divisions of time:*

3 *And even in the beginning of creation he makes mention of the sabbath. And God made in six days the work of his hands; and he finished them on the seventh day, and he rested the seventh day, and sanctified it.*

4 *Consider, my children, what that signifies, he finished them in six days. The meaning of it is this; that in six thousand years the Lord God will bring all things to an end. For with him, one day is as a thousand years. . .* (Epistle of Barnabas 13:3-5).

The *first* allegory was hidden within the six days in which God "labored." ***But the second allegory is revealed within the seventh or sabbath day, in which God "rested."***

Now we know that *"God is spirit. . ."* (John 4:24). And therefore His "labors" and His "rest" are both in the spirit. Dimensionless.

For example, the Scriptures emphatically set forth that, *"God said, 'Let there be light.'"* And light was!

And, *"God said, 'Let the waters under heaven be gathered together . . . and let the dry land appear;' and it was so."*

God spoke. And it simply came to be!

That is, He sent His Word. And in due course of time, it brought forth all that He declared.

No twenty-four hour periods. No literal six days. No labor. *Just His Word.*

But then God "rested." Having arbitrarily established a human time frame for Creation in order to help us understand His ways, **God is now explaining He has given us a corresponding literal period of time here on earth within which to enter His rest – that is, His spiritual rest.**

Just as "God rested on the seventh day and sanctified it," so now we are invited to share in His spiritual rest – having been sanctified by grace, that is, freed from sin and set apart for His sacred service.

To put it another way, the "seventh day" represents the allotted time you and I have been given on earth within which to cease from our labors *in the flesh* and find the way to fellowship with God through faith in Jesus Christ. *By following in the footsteps of Jesus, we can share His "sabbath rest" of peace and joy right here on earth,* living the rest of our lives not for ourselves, in bondage to the temporal pursuits of earthly "treasures," but set aside for His holy service.

For the Sabbath is not only a day of rest, *it is a way of life in which we live for the glory of God every day.*

Listen to the words of the New Testament *Book of Hebrews* as the author – whom many believe was also *Barnabas* – warns his readers against missing Christ's rest *today* because of disobedience – *just as the Israelites did in the days when Moses led them out of Egypt, and the entire generation wandered in the wilderness for forty years and perished there:*

1 Therefore, while the promise of entering his rest remains, let us fear lest any of you be judged to have failed to reach it.

2 For good news came to us just as to them; but the message they heard did not benefit them, because it did not meet with faith in the hearers.

3 For we who have believed enter that rest. . .

4 For he has somewhere spoken of the seventh day in this way, *"And God rested on the seventh day from all his works," . . . .*

6 Since therefore it remains for some to enter it, and those who formerly received the good news failed to enter because of disobedience,

7 again he sets a certain day. . . . *'Today when you hear his voice, do not harden your hearts." . . . .*

9 *So then, there remains a sabbath rest for the people of God;*

10 ***for whoever enters God's rest also ceases from his labors as God did from his*** (Heb. 4:1-4,6,7,9,10).

The wonderful story of Creation – indeed the whole Bible – was written just to tell you and me there is a place where we can go through faith in Christ today – back into the Garden of God's presence which was lost to Adam and Eve – and find rest for our souls.

APPENDIX

IN JUNE OF 2015 the United States Supreme Court bent the knee in the ultimate act of political expediency by holding, in a 5 – 4 decision, that the fundamental right to marry is guaranteed *even to same sex couples* by the Equal Protection Clause of the Fourteenth Amendment and the Due Process Clause.

But six thousand years earlier, another court, far superior to the United States Supreme Court, had already promulgated a different "decision." At the beginning of His Creation, Almighty God forever declared that He had created man *"In His own image . . . male and female He created them"* (Gen. 1:28).

And, *"He blessed them and said to them, 'Be fruitful and multiply and fill the earth. . . '"* (Gen. 1:28).

This is the first command from God to mankind in the Bible. Before all others in time and order, it was the cornerstone upon which life began, and upon which it has continued down through the ages.

Just two chapters before the end of the Old Testament (Malachi 2:15), God put His "seal" on what He had already made abundantly clear at the beginning, saying, *"Has not the Lord made them one? In flesh and spirit they are his. And why one? Because He was seeking godly offspring."*

Almighty God, in order to create for Himself a holy family of sons and daughters on Earth, created man in His image – male and female – that they might bring forth "godly offspring!" To violate this natural and holy foundation is to utterly destroy the familial bedrock upon which society rests. *The result is irremediable chaos.*

And he said to me, *"These words are trustworthy and true. And the Lord, the God of the Spirits of the prophets, has sent his angel to show his servants what must soon take place."*

Revelation 22:6

2070
The Neill's
P. O. Box 86
Athens, TN 37371